DC M...
Strai...

Based on the motion picture *Humpday*,
written and directed by Lynn Shelton

Methuen Drama

Published by Methuen Drama

Methuen Drama, an imprint of Bloomsbury Publishing Plc

1 3 5 7 9 10 8 6 4 2

Methuen Drama
Bloomsbury Publishing Plc
50 Bedford Square
London WC1B 3DP
www.methuendrama.com

Based on the motion picture *Humpday*,
written and directed by Lynn Shelton

ISBN 978 1 408 18463 9

A CIP catalogue record for this book is available from the British Library

Available in the USA from Bloomsbury Academic & Professional,
175 Fifth Avenue/3rd Floor, New York, NY 10010.

Typeset by Mark Heslington Ltd, Scarborough, North Yorkshire

A Sheffield Theatres Production
In association with the Bush Theatre

Straight

by **DC Moore**

Based on the motion picture *Humpday*,
written and directed by Lynn Shelton

The first performance of **Straight** took place on Thursday
1 November 2012 at the Crucible Studio Theatre, Sheffield

Straight
By **DC Moore**

Based on the motion picture *Humpday*, written and directed by Lynn Shelton

Cast

Waldorf	Philip McGinley
Lewis	Henry Pettigrew
Steph	Jenny Rainsford
Morgan	Jessica Ransom

Creative Team

Director	Richard Wilson
Designer	James Cotterill
Lighting Designer	Johanna Town
Composer	Michael Bruce
Assistant Director	Jon Pashley
Casting Director	Robert Sterne CDG

Stage Manager	Sarah Gentle
Deputy Stage Manager	Kirsty Louise Airlie
Assistant Stage Manager	Lucy Topham

Sets and costumes by Sheffield Theatres' workshop and wardrobe departments

This production is supported by HILL DICKINSON
LAWYERS

Cast Biographies

PHILIP McGINLEY Waldorf

Philip's theatre credits include *Herding Cats* (Theatre Royal Bath/Hampstead Theatre); *Hobson's Choice* (Crucible Theatre, Sheffield); *Canary* (Liverpool Everyman/ Hampstead Theatre); *More Light* (Arcola Theatre); *The Changeling* (Cheek by Jowl European tour); *Great Expectations* (Royal Shakespeare Company); *Kes* (Royal Exchange Theatre).

Television credits include *Game of Thrones, The Gemma Factor, Coronation Street, The Bill, Casualty, Cold Blood, Heartbeat, Blue Murder, Falling, Battlefield Britain, Hawking, The Deputy* and *Dalziel and Pascoe*.

His film credits include *Prometheus* and *Tested*.

HENRY PETTIGREW Lewis

Henry trained at Guildhall.

Henry's theatre credits include *The Master and Margarita* (Complicite); *Anna Christie* (Donmar); *Beautiful Burnout* (Frantic Assembly/National Theatre of Scotland); *Hamlet* (Donmar Broadway, Donmar West End); *Black Watch* (National Theatre of Scotland tour, Barbican, New York, Los Angeles); *The Bevellers* (Glasgow) and *Troilus and Cressida* (Edinburgh International Festival, Royal Shakespeare Company Stratford).

His television credits include *Doctors, The Relief of Belsen* and *Midsomer Murders*.

Radio credits include *The Family Man* and *The Sun at Midnight*.

JENNY RAINSFORD Steph

Jenny graduated from RADA in 2011 and has a degree in English Literature from Oxford University.

Her theatre credits include *The Importance of Being Earnest* (The Rose Theatre); *Our Town, The Crucible, Splendour, Oh! What a Lovely War, Othello, The Maid's Tragedy, Love for Love, Electra, Mr Norris Changes Trains* (RADA); *Ghosts* (Oxford University) and *Macbeth* (The English Speaking Union).

Jenny's film credits include *About Time, The Farmer* and *Prometheus*.

Jenny's television credits include *Da Vinci's Demons*.

JESSICA RANSOM Morgan

Jessica's theatre credits include *Posh* (Duke of York's/Royal Court); *Unsung Heroes, Ransom's Million* (Pleasance, Edinburgh); *Rogue Males, Field Study* (Edinburgh Festival); *The Wonder! A Woman Keeps a Secret* (Battersea Arts Centre).

Her film and television credits include *Saucerful of Secrets, Horrible Histories, Doc Martin, This is JLS Hidden Camera Projects, The Armstrong and Miller Show*. Radio credits include *This Time Next Week, Instant Rimshot, Idiots of Ants: Totally Gizmo* and *The Odd Half Hour*.

Jessica has written *I Was There Too* (Radio 4) and *The Armstrong and Miller Show*.

Creative Team Biographies

DC MOORE Playwright

DC Moore's plays include *Alaska* (Royal Court), *The Empire* (Royal Court and Drum Theatre, Plymouth, winner of the TMA Award for Best Touring Production), *Honest* (Royal & Derngate, Northampton, Edinburgh Festival & Soho Theatre), *Town* (Royal & Derngate, Northampton) and *The Swan* (as part of Double Feature – National Theatre, Paintframe). In 2008 he won the inaugural Tom Erhardt Award for promising new playwrights and was the 2011 Pearson Playwright in Residence at the Royal Court Theatre. He adapted *The Empire* for Radio 3's *The Wire* season and his television credits include *Home* for Channel 4/Touchpaper's 2011 Coming Up scheme.

RICHARD WILSON Director

Richard is a former Associate Director of the Royal Court Theatre and is currently an Associate Director for Sheffield Theatres where he directed *That Face* in 2010, *The Pride* starring Daniel Evans in 2011 and *Lungs* by Duncan Macmillan.

His recent stage work includes *Twelfth Night* (RSC) and *Whipping It Up* (The Bush Theatre).

His other directing credits include *Astronaut Wives Club* (National Youth Theatre); *Rainbow Kiss, The Woman Before, Under the Whaleback, A Day in Dull Armour/Graffiti, Where Do We Live, Nightingale and Chase, I Just Stopped to See the Man* and *Mr Kolpert* (Royal Court); *East Coast Chicken Supper* (Traverse); *Primo* (National Theatre/South Africa/Hampstead/Broadway); *Playing the Victim* (Sheffield/Traverse/Royal Court/tour); *Four Knights in Knaresborough* (New Vic Theatre Workshop for Tricycle); *Toast, Four* (Royal Court Theatre Upstairs); *Tom and Clem* (Tour/West End); *Simply Disconnected* (Chichester); *The Lodger* (Hampstead/Royal Exchange); *Women Laughing* (Royal Exchange/Royal Court, Manchester Evening News Best Play and Writers' Guild Award for Regional Theatres); *Imagine Drowning* (Hampstead, Winner John Whiting Award); *Prin* (Lyric Hammersmith); *A Wholly Healthy Glasgow* (Royal Exchange/Royal Court Edinburgh) *An Inspector Calls* (Royal Exchange, Manchester) and many more.

Richard has numerous television credits including *Merlin* and *One Foot in the Grave*.

In 1994 Richard was awarded the OBE for services to drama as a director and actor. From 1996 until 1999 he was Rector of Glasgow University. He is now the Visiting Professor for Drama at Glasgow University. He has honorary degrees from both Glasgow University and the University of Caledonia.

JAMES COTTERILL Designer

James's recent designs include *Good, A View from the Bridge, Powder Monkey, Mojo Mickybo* (Royal Exchange Theatre); *The Pride, That Face* (Crucible Studio); *The Seven Year Itch* (Salisbury Playhouse), *Macbeth; The Demolition Man* (Bolton Octagon), *Accolade* (Finborough Theatre), *The Flint Street Nativity, The Elves and the Shoemaker* (Hull Truck), *The Wages of Thin* (Old Red Lion) (Off West End.Com Nomination for Best Set), *Meat* (Theatre503); *Estate Walls* (Oval House). In 2005 he was a winner of the Linbury Prize for Stage Design for *Not the End of the World* at Bristol Old Vic. In 2009 his installation *Smash Here* was chosen by *Time Out* to be part of the Deloitte Ignite festival at the Royal Opera House.

Other designs include *The Eleventh Capital, Gone Too Far!* (Royal Court Upstairs); *A Little Neck* (Goat and Monkey at Hampton Court Palace); *The Musician* (OMAC, Belfast); *Lough/Rain* (Theatre Royal, York); *So Close to Home* (Arcola Theatre and Brighton Festival); *Spies* (Theatre Alibi, Oxford Playhouse and tour); *The Pleasure Principle* (Tristan Bates); *Romeo and Juliet* (BAC); *Big Sale* (Protein Dance/The Place and UK tour); *Fair* (Trafalgar Studio 2); *Silverland, 15 Minutes* (Arcola Theatre); *Widows, The Fool* (Vanbrugh Theatre, RADA).

JOHANNA TOWN Lighting Designer

Other productions for Sheffield Theatres include *The Pride* and *That Face*.

Recent theatre credits include *Blue Sky* (Pentabus); *Moon on a Rainbow Shawl* (National); *The Norman Conquests* (Liverpool); *Medea, Romeo and Juliet* (Headlong); *Blue Heart Afternoon, Lay Down Your Cross* (Hampstead); *What the Butler Saw, Betrayal, Speaking in Tongues, Fat Pig* (West End); *Some Like It Hip Hop* (ZooNation); *Charged* (Soho); *Miss Julie, Beautiful Thing, Private*

Lives, The Glass Menagerie, A Raisin in the Sun (Royal Exchange); Man in the Middle (503); The Deep Blue Sea/Nijinsky (Chichester); Fatherland (Gate); The Tragedy of Thomas Hobbes (RSC); Les Liaisons Dangereuses (Salisbury); Haunted (Royal Exchange/ New York); Romeo and Juliet, The Importance of Being Earnest (Edinburgh Lyceum). Productions for Out of Joint include Our Country's Good, Bang Bang Bang, Dreams of Violence, Our Lady of Sligo, The Permanent Way and King of Hearts. Extensive work with the Royal Court includes My Name is Rachel Corrie, Rhinoceros, The Arsonists and My Child.

MICHAEL BRUCE Composer

Michael's recent theatre work includes Berenice, Philadelphia, Here I Come!, The Physicists, The Recruiting Officer (Donmar); Relatively Speaking (National Tour); Blue Heart Afternoon (Hampstead Theatre Downstairs); Noises Off (Old Vic/West End); 24 Hour Plays (Old Vic); Sixty Six Books (Bush Theatre); Much Ado About Nothing (Sonia Friedman Productions/West End); Men Should Weep (National Theatre); The Great British Country Fete (National Tour/ Latitude Festival/The Bush Theatre); Christmas In New York (West End); Michael Bruce At The Apollo (West End); Ed: The Musical (Edinburgh Fringe); Holes (New Wimbledon Studio); Ed (Trafalgar Studios); Helen of Troy (Workshop, Little Angel Theatre Company) and Ruthie Henshall In Concert (The Guildhall, London).

Michael's television credits include The Alan Titchmarsh Show, Chita Rivera Special (Spun Gold TV) and the Confused.com adverts.

His radio credits include The Pied Piper and the Musicians of Bremen and The Grimm of Stottesdon Hall (The Wireless Theatre Company).

His recordings include Much Ado About Nothing (Sonia Friedman Productions); Unwritten Songs, Helena Blackman: The Sound of Rodgers & Hammerstein, Julie Atherton: No Space for Air, Christmas in New York (all Speculation Entertainment); Mark Evans: The Journey Home (Sain Records); Claudia Morris: Love and Demons (Album).

Michael was the first ever composer in residence at both the Bush Theatre and the Donmar Warehouse. He also received the Notes For The Stage Prize for songwriting.

JON PASHLEY Assistant Director

Credits as Assistant Director include *Macbeth* (Crucible Theatre, Sheffield); *A Marvellous Year for Plums, Rattigan's Nijinsky, The Deep Blue Sea* (Chichester Festival Theatre); *Someone Who'll Watch Over Me* (Southwark Playhouse); *Ashes and Sand, The House of Special Purpose* (RADA); *The Game of Love and Chance* (Salisbury Playhouse); *Toad of Toad Hall* (Rolls-Royce Motor Cars Goodwood) and *Coward, Cabaret and Cocktails – If Love Were All* (Minerva Theatre).

Directing credits at Warwick include *Comedy on a Station Platform* (also translator. Warwick Arts Centre Studio); *Much Ado about Nothing* (B2 Coventry's Belgrade Theatre); *Arcadia* and *A Passage to India* (CAPITAL Centre).

Jon is a resident assistant director at Sheffield Theatres and a student on the Birkbeck MFH Theatre Directing course.

ROBERT STERNE CDG Casting Director

Robert has been working as casting associate at Nina Gold Casting for the past seven years. He read English at New College, Oxford and is also a graduate of the Royal Academy of Dramatic Art.

As associate with Nina Gold Casting, Robert's feature film credits include *Les Miserables* directed by Tom Hooper; *Rush* directed by Ron Howard; *Prometheus* directed by Ridley Scott; *Jack the Giant Killer* directed by Bryan Singer; *Iron Lady* directed by Phyllida Lloyd; *The King' Speech* directed by Tom Hooper; *Attack the Block* directed by Joe Cornish; *Jane Eyre* directed by Cary Fukunaga; *Hot Fuzz* directed by Edgar Wright; *Nowhere Boy* directed by Sam Taylor Wood; *Bright Star* directed by Jane Campion; *Eastern Promises* by David Cronenberg and two of Mike Leigh's films *Happy-Go-Lucky* and *Another Year*. He also worked in India as Indian Casting Associate on *Eat Pray Love* directed by Ryan Murphy.

Most recent television casting director credits include two seasons of *Game of Thrones* for HBO, *The Home* for ITV, *Coup* and *The Devil's Whore* for Company Pictures/HBO, *Small Island* for BBC and the comedy series *Threesome, Friday Night Dinner Seasons I and II* and *Free Agents* for Big Talk Productions/Channel 4. Other casting associate credits include the second series of *Rome* for HBO, *John Adams* for HBO, *The Red Riding Trilogy* (1974, 1979 and 1983) for Channel 4/Revolution Films and The Crimson Petal *and the White* for BBC/Origin Pictures

Production Credits

Sheffield Theatres would like to thank the following for their support on the production of **Straight**:

Waitrose 3 Ecclesall Road, Sheffield. 0114 272 2027

Matt Badcock

Environcom Contact Mark Knight on 07939 805 130 or at mark.knight@environcom.co.uk

Beam Global

Bang and Olufsen of Sheffield nick@sykesvideo.co.uk

Nick Hayes

Howdens Joinery Co. 0114 243 6539 or sheffield@howdens.co.uk

The Bathroom Company www.sheffieldbathroomcompany.com

B. Munday Plumbing and Heating 07837 274 343

Pickfords Removals 0114 321 1300 or 0800 079 8557

TLJ Security Systems www.tlj-hotellocks.co.uk

Greatbeanbags.com www.greatbeanbags.com

 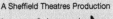

Sheffield Theatres

Sheffield Theatres is the largest producing theatre complex outside London. Across its three theatres: the Crucible, the Lyceum and the Studio, the company produces and presents a diverse programme of work including drama, dance, comedy, musicals, opera, ballet and children's shows.

The subject of a major redevelopment project, since reopening in 2010, the Crucible has re-established its reputation as one of the country's most important producing theatres. Over the last three years, the company has attracted widespread national and international interest for its productions including **An Enemy of the People** with **Sir Antony Sher**, **Hamlet** with **John Simm** in the title role, **Me and My Girl** – a major revival of the musical under the direction of **Anna Mackmin**, two playwrights seasons – one celebrating the work of **Sir David Hare** (2011) and the second celebrating the work of **Michael Frayn** (2012), **Othello** with **Clarke Peters** and **Dominic West**, **Stephen Sondheim**'s **Company** with Artistic Director **Daniel Evans** in the lead role of Bobby and most recently, **Macbeth** with **Geoffrey Streatfeild** and **Claudie Blakley**.

Two of the Theatres' productions have transferred to the capital this year: **Democracy** transferred to the Old Vic in June and the Roundabout Season, a co-production with Paines Plough, opened at Shoreditch Town Hall in September 2012. Next year Sheffield Theatres will co-produce the world premiere of **The Full Monty** which has been adapted for the stage by Oscar winning writer **Simon Beaufoy** and will then embark on a 10 week tour of the country.

Sheffield Theatres is delighted to be working with the Bush Theatre to stage the world premiere production of **Straight** by **DC Moore**. To find out more please visit sheffieldtheatres.co.uk

Chief Executive **Dan Bates**
Artistic Director **Daniel Evans**

A Sheffield Theatres Production

THE FULL MONTY
THE PLAY
BY SIMON BEAUFOY

Director **Daniel Evans**
Designer **Robert Jones**
Choreographer
Steven Hoggett
Lighting Designer
Tim Lutkin
Music and Sound
Ben and Max Ringham

Based on the Fox
Searchlight Pictures
motion picture

Lyceum Theatre

Sat 2 – Sat 23 February

Simon Beaufoy, the Oscar winning writer of the film, has gone back to Sheffield where it all started to rediscover the men, the women, the heartache and the hilarity of a city on the dole.

Cast includes: **Scott Anson, Tracy Brabin, Kieran O'Brien, Caroline Carver, Sidney Cole, Eamonn Fleming, Craig Gazey, Elaine Glover, Rachel Lumberg, Ian Mercer, Roger Morlidge and Simon Rouse.**

Tickets available now from £9.00 – £30.00

BUSH THEATRE

About the Bush

The Bush Theatre is a world-famous home for new plays and an internationally renowned champion of playwrights and artists. Since its inception in 1972, the Bush has pursued its singular vision of discovery, risk and entertainment from a distinctive corner of West London. Now located in a recently renovated library building on the Uxbridge Road in the heart of Shepherds Bush, the theatre houses a 144-seat auditorium, rehearsal rooms and a lively café bar.

www.bushtheatre.co.uk

THANK YOU
TO OUR SUPPORTERS

The Bush Theatre would like to extend a very special 'Thank You' to the following Patrons, Corporate Supporters and Trusts & Foundations whose valuable contributions continue to help us nurture, develop and present some of the brightest new literary stars and theatre artists.

LONE STAR

Gianni Alen-Buckley
Michael Alen-Buckley
Steffanie Brown
Francois & Julie Buclez
Siri & Rob Cope
Jonathan Ford & Susannah Herbert
Catherine Johnson
Caryn Mandabach
Miles Morland
Lady Susie Sainsbury
James & Virginia Turnbull
Nicholas & Francesca Whyatt

HANDFUL OF STARS

Anonymous
Micaela Boas
Jim Broadbent
Philip & Tita Byrne
Sarah Cooke
Clyde Cooper
Irene Danilovich
David & Alexandra Emmerson
Catherine Faulks
Chris & Sofia Fenichell
Kate Groes
Simon Johnson
Paul Kafka
Nicolette Kirkby
Pierre Lagrange & Roubi L'Roubi
Mark & Sophie Lewisohn
Adrian & Antonia Lloyd
Eugenie White & Andrew Loewenthal
Scott & Laura Malkin
Peter & Bettina Mallinson
Paige Nelson
Georgia Oetker
Bianca Roden
Claudia Rossler
Naomi Russell
Charles & Emma Sanderson
Joana & Henrik Schliemann
Jon & NoraLee Sedmak
Larus Shields
Trish Wadley
Charlotte & Simon Warshaw
John & Amelia Winter

RISING STARS

Anonymous
Melanie Aram
Nick Balfour
Tessa Bamford
David Bernstein & Sophie Caruth
Simon & Lucy Berry
John Bottrill
David Brooks
Karen Brost
Maggie Burrows
Clive Butler
Matthew Byam Shaw
Benedetta Cassinelli
Tim & Andrea Clark
Claude & Susie Cochin de Billy
Angela Cole
Matthew Cushen
Michael & Marianne de Giorgio

RISING STARS CONTINUED

Yvonna Demczynska
Alexandra Eagle
Charles Emmerson
Jane & David Fletcher
Lady Antonia Fraser
Sylvie Freund-Pickavance
Vivien Goodwin
Sarah Griffin
Hugh & Sarah Grootenhuis
Mr & Mrs Jan Gustafsson
Martin & Melanie Hall
Sarah Hall
Giselle Hantz
Giles Haughton
Hugo & Julia Heath
Urs & Alice Hodler
Bea Hollond
Zaza Jabre
Philip Jones
Ann & Ravi Joseph
Davina & Malcolm Judelson
Rupert Jolley & Aine Kelly
Kristen Kennish
Heather Killen
Sue Knox
Kirsty Lang
Caroline Mackay
Isabella Macpherson
Charlie & Polly McAndrew
Michael McCoy
Judith Mellor
Caro Millington
Miles Montgomerie
Kate Pakenham
Kevin Pakenham
Denise Parkinson
Mark & Anne Paterson
Julian & Amanda Platt
Lila Preston
Radfin Courier Service
Kirsty Raper
Clare Rich
Joanna Richards
Sarah Richards
Robert Rooney
Karen Scofield & LUCZA
Russ Shaw & Lesley Hill
Saleem & Alexandra Siddiqi
Melanie Slimmon
Brian Smith
William Smith-Bowers
Sebastian & Rebecca Speight
Nick Starr
Andrew & Emma Sutcliffe
The Uncertainty Principle
Ed Vaizey
Marina Vaizey
The van Tulleken family
Francois & Arelle von Hurter
Hilary Vyse & Mark Ellis
Amanda Waggott
Dame Harriet Walter
Peter Wilson-Smith & Kat Callo
Alison Winter
Jessica Zambeletti

CORPORATE SUPPORTERS

SPOTLIGHT

John Lewis, Park Royal
Walt Disney & Co Ltd

LIGHTBULB

The Agency (London) Ltd
AKA
Mozzo Coffee & La Marzocco
Talk Talk Ltd

The Bush would also like to thank **Markson Pianos, Westfield** and **West 12 Shopping & Leisure Centre**

We would also like to thank **Ogilvy & Mather** for sponsoring FEAR

TRUSTS AND FOUNDATIONS

The Andrew Lloyd Webber Foundation
The Daisy Trust
The D'Oyly Carte Charitable Trust
EC&O Venues Charitable Trust
The Elizabeth & Gordon Bloor Charitable Foundation
Foundation for Sport and the Arts
Garfield Weston Foundation
Garrick Charitable Trust
The Gatsby Charitable Foundation
The Goldsmiths' Company
The Harold Hyam Wingate Foundation
Jerwood Charitable Foundation
The John Thaw Foundation
The Laurie & Gillian Marsh Charitable Trust
The Leverhulme Trust
The Martin Bowley Charitable Trust
The Thistle Trust
The Worshipful Company of Grocers
Sir Siegmund Warburg's Voluntary Settlement

PUBLIC FUNDING

Supported by
ARTS COUNCIL ENGLAND

putting residents first

If you are interested in finding out how to be involved, please visit the 'Support Us' section of www.bushtheatre.co.uk, email development@bushtheatre.co.uk or call 020 8743 3584

Straight

Characters

Lewis
Morgan
Waldorf
Steph

Notes on the text
This play can be performed with or without décor.

If performed with décor, Part One should look messy, crammed and brimming with stuff/life; Part Two should look sparse, spacious and light.

If performed without décor, there is no need to explicitly mime or act out any of the action. Unless you want to.

Dialogue in the play can, and probably should, be changed, here and there, to reflect: i) the physicality (age/ethnicity/size, etc.) of the actors; ii) the specifics of any décor used, if any; and, iii) any changes in the political/social/cultural landscape that might date references in the play, or distance us from it (in whatever manner). It is set now. And should feel as now and alive and as present tense as you can possibly make it.

Part One

Scene One

Lewis *and* **Morgan**.

Lewis   Yeah, yeah. Fuck. You know?

Morgan   Yeah.

Silence.

Lewis   (Will it fit?)

Morgan   What?

Lewis   . . .

Morgan   What you say?

Lewis   Nothing.

Morgan   You did.

Lewis   Didn't.

Morgan   I heard you.

Lewis   Erm, I've forgotten.

Morgan   You haven't though.

Lewis   I have.

Morgan   You literally haven't.

Lewis   Alright, but still.

Morgan   What?

Lewis   . . . I dunno, now.

Morgan   What?

Lewis   I've sort of lost the thread of what I was . . .

Morgan   Oh my God just say it just say what you said just then you fucking knobhead.

Lewis   . . . alright. Alright.

Morgan   Lewis.

Lewis   Yeah. Will it fit?

Morgan   What?

Lewis   A kid. 'In here.'

Morgan   Course.

Lewis   A whole one?

Morgan   Yeah.

Lewis   How?

Morgan   Easy.

Lewis   You seen how big they get?

Morgan   Flats?

Lewis   Children.

Morgan   Yeah.

Lewis   So where then?

Morgan   Oven.

Lewis   Right.

Morgan   Got a little, inbuilt timer, for an alarm. Window, to look out. Just whack a towel in, for a carpet: job done.

Lewis   What about when we cook?

Morgan   Take her out.

Lewis   Her?

Morgan   Him. Her. It. Them. Yeah.

Lewis   What if the door shuts? Be airtight.

Morgan   No, coz it's fan-assisted.

Lewis   (You're fan-assisted.)

Morgan   (Clever.)

Lewis   (You're . . . clever.)

Morgan   (Yeah.)

Pause.

Lewis   What ya doing?

Morgan   What?

Lewis   On your phone.

Morgan   Nothing. Just. E-mails.

Lewis   Work?

Morgan   No.

Lewis   Work?

Morgan   Yeah.

Lewis   What?

Morgan   Prep stuff.

Lewis   Have I not . . . ?

Morgan   Done soon.

Lewis   Yeah?

Morgan   Yeah, then bed.

Lewis   ('Sweet.') Will you really, though?

Morgan   Yeah.

Lewis   OK.

Silence.

Lewis   We might need a soundtrack.

Morgan   Lewis.

Lewis   Sorry.

Morgan   You need to sort out your timing. Do 'em at work. Seriously.

Lewis   I know. But you don't always . . . hold them in. Either.

Morgan   . . .

Lewis   'Do ya?'

Music.

Morgan   Alright?

Lewis   Yeah, we might need something a bit more. Raucous.

Different music.

Morgan   Better?

Lewis   Yep. 'Thank you guv.'

Morgan   'S'alright my son.'

Lewis *exits.*

Morgan   Why do you always lock it?

Lewis (*off*)   What?

Morgan   Toilet door.

Lewis (*off*)   Can't really hear you!

Morgan   (No.)

Pause.

Lewis *enters.*

Lewis   Where's the paper?

Morgan   What?

Lewis Toilet?

Morgan Oh. Sorry.

Lewis Could you chuck it me?

Morgan Yeah.

Lewis Ta.

Lewis *exits*.

Pause.

Morgan Oh, er. Lewis. *Lewis! LEWIS!*

Lewis (*off*) What?

Morgan Would ya . . . would you come out please!

Lewis (*off*) Why? I've only just . . .

Morgan There's a . . .

Lewis (*off*) What?

Morgan . . . in the . . .

Lewis (*off*) What are you saying?

Morgan Just come out, would you, yeah?

Lewis (*off*) Alright. Yep. Just a second!

Pause.

Lewis *enters*.

Lewis Sorry, I couldn't really hear you over the . . .

Music off.

Lewis What's wrong?

Morgan Yeah, there was erm . . . I don't really know how to say this but there was a, a penis in the . . .

Lewis What?

Morgan . . . letterbox.

Lewis   OK.

Morgan   And it was all . . .

Lewis   What?

Morgan   . . . jiggling . . .

Lewis   Jiggling . . . ?

Morgan   Yeah jiggling around yeah moving around to the, to the music.

Lewis   Our music?

Morgan   Yeah. And then it . . . went.

Lewis   OK.

Morgan   Honestly.

Lewis   Right. An actual like physical, like, knob?

Morgan   Yeah. Are you gonna go and . . . ?

Lewis   Yeah. OK. I will. Right. But . . . OK. Was it like . . . erect then, or?

Morgan   No.

Lewis   So he wasn't like touching it through the . . . ? There wasn't any . . . ?

Morgan   What?

Lewis   . . . product?

Morgan   No.

Lewis   Great. But it was a . . . ?

Morgan   Yeah.

Lewis   Right.

Morgan   Honestly, are you gonna check then or . . . ?

Lewis   Yeah yeah, I just wanna be, you know. Prepared. I mean, did he look, angry, or?

Morgan   It was difficult to tell, really.

Lewis   Right. Well I'll take a saucepan then. In case. He was.

Morgan   OK.

Lewis *exits*.

Silence.

Lewis *enters*.

Lewis   No one.

Morgan   Really?

Lewis   Yeah. Lift's not moving. Hallway's empty. No sound from any of the other flats.

Morgan   OK.

Lewis   Mystery.

Morgan   I didn't make it up.

Lewis   I know.

Morgan   Should we call the police?

Lewis   No. Should we?

Morgan   I don't know.

Lewis   Yeah I mean it's probably just. You know, like students from one of the sub-lets upstairs, or, something.

Morgan   Yeah, I suppose, it wasn't really all that threatening, really. Quite silly. Bobbling about.

Lewis   Was it not very big?

Morgan   I don't know, it was floppy.

Lewis   Right but was it suggestive of a larger man's . . . ?

Morgan   Lewis, that's not really the . . .

Lewis   OK. And was it. You know . . . ?

Morgan   What?

Lewis   . . . white?

Morgan   Yes.

Lewis   OK. (*Pause*.) Are you alright?

Morgan   Fine.

Lewis   Sure?

Morgan   Yeah, seen enough o' them. To not be too . . . fazed, or whatever. Jesus Christ, what have you been eating?

Lewis   Yeah sorry, I'll get the extractor on.

Lewis *exits*.

Morgan   (Appreciated, captain.)

Pause.

Lewis *enters*.

Lewis   You look a bit pale.

Morgan   You sure there was no one out there?

Lewis   Yeah.

Morgan   What if he like attacks someone?

Lewis   What, with his cock?

Morgan   Yeah, that is what happens.

Lewis   Erm, I don't know.

Morgan   I'm gonna call 'em.

Lewis   Police?

Morgan   Yeah.

Lewis   OK but what are they gonna do? Finger-print the . . . ? I mean, if he lives here, then he's probably hiding in his own flat now. And if he's not, he's probably run off.

Morgan   Alright, well maybe I'll e-mail the Neighbourhood Police Team, or something.

Lewis   Right. 'Good plan, cap'n.'

Morgan   I'll do it now.

Lewis   Cool. Responsible. Mature.

Silence.

Lewis   You found the site OK?

Morgan   Yeah. Doing it now.

Lewis   I love that you can type and talk. And at least the extractor's working now. Sort of. You just have to pull it down really hard and then sort of jiggle it and punch it, repeatedly.

Morgan   Right.

Silence.

Morgan   Why do you always lock it?

Lewis   What?

Morgan   Toilet.

Lewis   I dunno: habit.

Morgan   But you know that I know you're in there.

Lewis   Yeah, but . . .

Morgan   What?

Lewis   . . . well, I think it's because I once saw my mum having a, a dump. In a field.

Morgan   Shit.

Lewis   Yeah. We were on a big walk in the Dales. My dad was helping her out with the improvising. Leaves and stuff. He'd told us to stay at the bottom of it – the field – near these bushes. But I wanted to know what they were doing. So I wandered up, all innocent. And erm . . . yeah.

Morgan   How old were you?

Lewis   Eight.

Morgan   Flip.

Lewis   Yeah.

Morgan   I've not seen either of my parents defecate.

Lewis   It stays with you.

Morgan   And that's why you still lock it? Honestly?

Lewis   Think so.

Morgan   That's sort of cute.

Lewis   Is it?

Morgan   Yeah.

Lewis   And if we do it. One day, oven boy will have to watch us having a massive shit in a field, too. Probably. And that's sort of. Terrifying. Isn't it?

Morgan   Course it is. That's the point.

Silence.

Lewis   I do love you, dickhead.

Morgan   I love you too you big fat hairy cocksucker. Right. It's sent. I suppose that's all we can do now, isn't it?

Lewis   Yeah. Do you wanna come here?

Morgan   What, cock through the door got you horny, has it?

Lewis   Yeah.

Morgan   He might still be out there. Lurking.

Lewis   I don't care.

Morgan   OK, but before we get all . . . I've got a meeting tomorrow morning that I haven't really prepared for.

Lewis   I'll give you a meeting tomorrow morning that you haven't really prepared for.

Morgan   Shut up.

Lewis   I'll shut you up.

Morgan   That doesn't really mean anything.

Lewis   I'll make you not really mean anything.

Morgan   Stop it.

Lewis   Come on: fuck the meeting.

Morgan   . . . OK.

Lewis   Yeah?

Morgan   Yeah.

Lewis   And I won't wear one?

Morgan   No.

Lewis   Sure?

Morgan   Yeah. We said.

Lewis   Yeah, I just wanted to be . . .

Morgan   Sure?

Lewis   Yeah. Coz I am.

Morgan   Yeah?

Lewis   Yeah. I think. And is the monthly dangerzone volcano stuff alright?

Morgan   *'Just about, squire.'*

Lewis   OK. You know . . .

Morgan   What?

Lewis   I want you to think about this during your meeting.

Morgan   OK.

Lewis   It's all I want you to think about.

Morgan   OK.

Lewis   Us.

Morgan   Yeah.

Lewis   Me, inside you.

Morgan   OK. Yeah.

Lewis   I love you.

Morgan   I love you.

Silence.

Morgan   *Oh . . . erm!*

Lewis   *What what what did I . . . ?* Did I hurt you?

Morgan   No no: it's . . . it's back.

Lewis   What? The . . . ?

Morgan   Yeah.

Lewis   Fuck.

Morgan   I told you (!).

Lewis   Jesus Christ. Right, yeah fuck, I'm sorry mate, but you can't really do that, yeah? That's not really like allowed, or whatever. We're gonna call the fucking police now, OK?

Waldorf (*off*)   *'But I am the law!'*

Lewis   What?

Waldorf (*off*)   'I am the law.'

Lewis   No, say that again.

Waldorf (*off*)   I am. The law (?).

Lewis   Is that . . . ?

Waldorf (*off*)   Yeah.

Morgan   What?

Waldorf *enters*.

Waldorf   *Alright, you great cunt!*

Lewis   . . . hello fuck!

Morgan   You . . . know him?

Lewis   Yeah.

Waldorf   Mate.

Lewis   Christ.

Waldorf   Yeah.

Lewis   Fucking hell, well come here then you big daft . . .

Waldorf   Yeah. Fuck (!). '*Mother!*'

Lewis   Yeah. '*Mother!*'

Morgan   So are you gonna . . . ?

Lewis   Oh yeah yeah sorry fuck this is: Waldorf.

Morgan   Waldorf?

Waldorf   Yep.

Morgan   That's quite an entrance.

Waldorf   I know, yeah.

Morgan   Yeah, and are you gonna like . . . ?

Lewis   Oh yeah yeah yeah sorry this my sort of, no my actual: wife.

Morgan   Called?

Lewis   Morgan.

Waldorf   Morgan. 'Guten. Morgan.'

Morgan   Yeah, Morgan, yeah.

Waldorf   Sounds like. Mahogany, you know?

Morgan   What?

Waldorf   You know sounds like a solid bit of wood, you could use for like a fucking shelving unit or something. 'A Morgan.'

Morgan   Does it?

Waldorf   Yeah. In a good way though. Compliment.

Morgan   Right. So do you always enter a room cock-first, then?

Waldorf   Mostly, yeah. I'd doublefuck a nice cold beer, mate.

Lewis   Alright.

Morgan   Well. Welcome, I suppose. Both of you.

Lewis   Yeah. So God, where are you living now?

Waldorf   Here.

Lewis   What?

Waldorf   Well, you said that I could stay for a bit.

Lewis   Waldorf.

Waldorf   Yeah?

Lewis   I've not seen you in like, six or seven years mate.

Waldorf   Yeah but. Yeah, but. Yeah. But. *Yeah*. But. Before I left – yeah? – we had a nice little coffee and you said, when I got back, that I could crash at yours till I got like all settled 'n' that.

Lewis   No I didn't.

Waldorf   You really fucking did.

Lewis   OK but I think that was probably just one of those things you sort of say but don't really like, mean.

Waldorf   What: lies?

Lewis   No. Well. Sort of, yeah.

Waldorf   I've been travelling for seventy-eight hours, fucking, straight, here mate.

Lewis   You should have e-mailed me then or . . .

Waldorf   It's alright, you know, just give me the smallest bedroom, tonight. And I'll go tomorrow, first thing. Honestly. I'll be off like. Yoghurt. In a bin.

Morgan   There aren't any.

Waldorf   Bins?

Morgan   No, we've got plenty of bins. Bedrooms. This is it. Apart from the toilet shower thing.

Waldorf   What?

Lewis   This is the whole flat, Waldorf.

Morgan   Yeah.

Waldorf   No.

Lewis   Yeah.

Waldorf   Fuck off (!).

Morgan   Do you not notice that the bed is in the same room as the kitchen?

Waldorf   I thought that was a design choice.

Morgan   It is.

Lewis   Yeah.

Waldorf   Right. Wow. Well, I'll. Maybe I'll go then.

Lewis   Morgan?

Morgan   What?

Waldorf   No, it's OK. It's fine. Seriously mate. Only seven years, it's not like . . .

Morgan   How do you two even know each other?

Lewis   Oh yeah. Shit. Uni. We were best mates.

Waldorf   Are.

Lewis   Yeah, we *are* best mates, yeah.

Morgan   Oh, right. Well that makes a bit more sense.

Waldorf   Did he not mention me?

Lewis   No, I did, didn't I? Definitely.

Morgan   You must have, yeah (?).

Waldorf   Alright. Well. You know, I'll leave you to it then. I'm sorry to have . . .

Morgan   Where have you travelled from? Big enough rucksack.

Waldorf   Train station, town.

Morgan   No, like, before that?

Waldorf   Stansted.

Morgan   And before that?

Waldorf   Dubai. Stop-over.

Morgan   And that?

Waldorf   Korea.

Morgan   Really?

Waldorf   Yeah. A little village called Namsangol Hanok. Was beautiful.

Morgan   Wow. So what you've been travelling for like three days or whatever?

Waldorf   Pretty much.

Morgan   You must be totally knackered.

Waldorf   I am, yeah.

Morgan   And don't you have family to see?

Waldorf   . . . no I don't, really . . .

Morgan   What?

Waldorf   . . . get on with the . . .

Lewis   Yeah, he doesn't . . .

Waldorf   . . . no. I don't . . .

Morgan   OK.

Waldorf   So like I say yeah, maybe I'll go then, yeah?

Morgan   But where are you gonna go? Late now.

Waldorf   Somewhere. Anywhere, I dunno. Improvise.

Morgan   Well you know, obviously, like I say, you can stay here tonight, if you're a friend, obviously. I'm not a cunt.

Waldorf   No?

Morgan   Am I, Lewis?

Lewis   What?

Morgan   A cunt.

Lewis   No. Not at all.

Morgan   See? So, you know: have the sofa tonight, or. Please. You're welcome. It all sort of folds out. Just don't try and stick your penis through it (!). Or through anything else (!). Unless you want to.

Waldorf   No, I'm alright. Seriously, I hate imposing on people. I'm just not like that, you know?

Lewis   Waldorf.

Waldorf   Alright I will stay then thank you very much.

Lewis   Good.

Morgan   Cool.

Lewis   Yeah.

Pause.

Waldorf   Are there really no other rooms?

Lewis   No.

Waldorf   Awesome.

Morgan   Can I get you any food or anything?

Waldorf   No, I'm alright, ta. And what, so you both like own this place do you? Like, fucking proper adults 'n' that?

Lewis   Yeah.

Waldorf   '*Sweet.*'

Morgan   Yeah, it's ours, yeah.

Lewis   (Unfortunately.)

Morgan   (Don't say that.)

Waldorf   Why, what's wrong with it? Asbestos?

Lewis   No, not much, really.

Waldorf   Damp? Rats!

Morgan   No. We just paid slightly over. What we should have.

Waldorf   How much?

Lewis   Go on. I don't think I can actually say it.

Morgan   Well. We paid a hundred and ninety-eight thousand.

Waldorf   Pounds?

Morgan   Yeah. 2007. Top of the market. And everyone was . . . Weren't they? So we thought . . . And then it all went . . .

Lewis   Yeah.

Morgan   Fuck.

Waldorf   So what's it worth now?

Morgan   . . . forty-eight thousand, less.

Waldorf   And that's pounds again, is it?

Morgan   Yeah.

Waldorf   *'You fucking cunnnnntttts!'*

Lewis   I know.

Morgan   Yeah.

Waldorf   Well it's . . . lovely.

Lewis   Thank you.

Morgan   We weren't even gonna live here. (God.) Was an investment, really. We started renting it out. Then the rental market round here went . . . And it stopped covering the mortgage and then . . .

Lewis   So we didn't really have a choice.

Morgan   No, had to move in, few months back. Still getting used to it, really. Miss the old place, a lot.

Waldorf   Honestly, it's . . . brilliant.

Morgan   Bit cramped.

Waldorf   *No.* Cosy. Sort o' New York slash Tokyo slash Vegas, vibe.

Lewis   Thank you.

Morgan   Yeah.

Lewis   (You big fat lying prick.)

Morgan   So where else have you been then, other than Korea? Seven years (!).

Waldorf   Most places East, really, yeah. Nepal. Japan.
Thailand. Laos. India. Cambodia. Sri Lanka. Few of the
-stans. China. Vietnam. Philippines. Cook Islands. Georgia.
Fiji. Ethiopia, very briefly. Nearly Sudan but probably best
that fell through, really. Russia. Poland.

Morgan   So you're like a proper fucking adventurer, then?

Waldorf   I wouldn't say that but you can, yeah.

Morgan   What's the furthest you've been since he left?

Lewis   . . . Cumbria.

Waldorf   Wow.

Morgan   He's so brave.

Lewis   Suck my balls.

Waldorf   *'With pleasure, Jonathan!'*

Morgan   Right. Well. Anyway, sorry but . . .

Lewis   Yeah, it is a bit late now.

Morgan   School night. Do you mind if we sort of carry on
tomorrow, is that OK?

Waldorf   No yeah, not at all. I'm fucking obliterated,
anyway. Fucking jetlag like a motherfucking blaaaarggh
motherfucker. You know?

Lewis   Yeah.

Morgan   Great.

Lewis   And we can get you in a Travel Lodge or something
in the morning. And don't worry about the money, we'll
chip in.

Morgan   Will we?

Lewis   Yeah.

Morgan   OK. Fab.

Lewis And then we'll all go for a drink tomorrow night, or something. Catch up. Properly.

Waldorf Course. Yeah.

Morgan Great. I'm just useless without a good night's sleep, you know?

Waldorf Yeah, me too. But don't worry, I will be so quiet tonight, you'll be able to hear yourself menstruate. Both of you.

Morgan Brilliant.

Lewis Well. 'Welcome back you son of a gun!'

Waldorf 'Indubitably, sir! Indubitably!'

Morgan Oh, right. You do the voices thing, too.

Lewis Yeah. A bit. We used to, yeah.

Morgan I thought that was . . . just us.

Lewis Well, er . . . No.

Scene Two

Steph, *alone*.

Lewis *enters*.

Steph Hey.

Lewis . . . hey.

Steph You alright?

Lewis . . . yeah.

Steph Nice one. Wanna drink?

Lewis I'm already quite pissed, actually. Had a few at our desks for someone's birthday.

Steph Oh.

Lewis   Yeah. Sorry, but you're in my flat (?).

Steph   Oh right yeah I am yeah.

Lewis   Yeah, so why . . . are you?

Steph   Just chilling out relaxing, all cool, playing some b-ball, outside of. School.

Lewis   Yeah, are you smoking erm . . . ?

Steph   Yeah, do you want some?

Lewis   No, I am just gonna open a window though, if that's alright?

Steph   Course, yeah. Go like, nuts.

Lewis   . . . yeah.

Silence.

Lewis   Should I ask you again, then?

Steph   Go for it.

Lewis   Why are you in my flat?

Steph   Coz I'm like a fucking . . . yeah. What's the word?

Lewis   I don't know.

Steph   Oh, it's erm like . . . What is it? (*Pause.*) Burglar. Yeah. I'm like a fucking, burglar. And you've been totally sort of, like . . .

Lewis   Burgled?

Steph   Yeah. Not really. Waldorf sort of . . .

Lewis   How do you know him?

Steph   Yeah yeah sorry we met in the erm . . . (*Pause.*) Shop. You know, the shop that sells all the . . . stuff.

Lewis   Stuff?

Steph   Yeah we met in the shop that sells all the stuff and he bought me a Kit Kat Chunky and I said like thank you, for the Kit Kat Chunky, and then it just sort of like. Mushroomed.

Lewis   So he's not in a Travel Lodge?

Steph   No. Unless this is a Travel Lodge? It's not, is it?

Lewis   No.

Steph   Right. Cool. Yeah. You OK? You just seem a bit like fucked off, or whatever.

Lewis   No.

Steph   With me or whatever?

Lewis   Yeah, no no no, I'm not, no. Just Waldorf always does this.

Steph   What?

Lewis   Well the flat was clean when I left this morning. And it also – no offence – had only one woman in it, which was my. You know. Fucking. Wife.

Steph   Congratulations.

Lewis   Thank you.

Steph   I hope you're really like, happy together.

Lewis   We are, yeah.

Steph   Yeah?

Lewis   Yeah. Why wouldn't we be?

Steph   No reason.

Lewis   No, you said that like we wouldn't be. Why not?

Steph   I dunno.

Lewis   You can say it.

Steph   Yeah. Just like most people who like kill people are literally like the ones who are like married to them. And then like, if you don't, you have to like, wait there, and watch them die, like, slowly. Unless you like, leave, to watch someone else die, like, slowly.

Lewis   I suppose that's all technically correct.

Steph   And also, like no offence. But you seem a bit, I dunno.

Lewis   What?

Steph   Like Michael Gove, or someone. The Education . . .

Lewis   Yeah, I know who Michael Gove is.

Steph   Yeah, so do I. And I just always think he looks so, you know – on the television on 'Newsnight' – he always looks so unhappy. Like he's never really had like a hug. Or a real like human relationship. With like a person.

Lewis   OK, well I'm not like Michael Gove, so . . .

Steph   OK.

Lewis   I'm not.

Steph   Right.

Lewis   What?

Steph   Well, I don't think that even Michael Gove thinks he's like Michael Gove. I think that's like totally the point.

Lewis   . . . OK.

Steph   You know?

Lewis   Yeah. Alright, well I'm sorry, it's obviously not your fault that Waldorf is a . . . And I shouldn't be taking it out on you, just coz you're here. In my flat. Getting stoned.

Steph   That's alright.

Lewis   So yeah I'll try to be less Govey and more like erm
Chuka Umunna, or someone.

Steph   Who's that?

Lewis   The Shadow Secretary of State for Business,
Innovation and Skills.

Steph   He sounds really relaxed.

Lewis   He is. Because he's never had to deal with the
consequences of real power. (*Pause.*) Is that skunk?

Steph   Yeah.

Lewis   OK.

Steph   You still don't seem that like. Calm, or whatever.

Lewis   Where is he now, Waldorf?

Steph   The shop that sells all the . . .

Lewis   Stuff, yeah.

Steph   So are you not used to having like random women
in your flat then?

Lewis   Not really.

Steph   It's alright, I'm not gonna jump you, or anything.

Lewis   . . . OK.

Steph   Am I?

Lewis   No. What's your name, by the way?

Steph   Steph.

Lewis   Lewis.

Steph   As in like 'Lewis' on TV?

Lewis   Yeah, as in 'Morse', ITV, all that.

Steph   I used to think I was named after like Stephanie
Beacham but it turned out: I wasn't.

Lewis   OK.

Steph   But I told everyone at school I was, so that was . . .
(Yeah.) Though no one knew who she was anyway, so . . .

Pause.

Lewis   Did he say how long he'd be, at the shop?

Steph   No.

Lewis   Right. What's the skunk like?

Steph   Really sweet, yeah. Like, lingers.

Lewis   Could I have some?

Steph   Course.

Lewis   Ta. Ooh. That's. Lovely.

Steph   Canadian. They really know how to like erm . . .

Lewis   Obviously.

Steph   So were you named like after Morse then, or
his mate?

Lewis   No. Look, I'm really sorry for being all . . .

Steph   S'alright.

Lewis   Yeah, I'm basically saying, 'I'm not that much of a
dick but obviously I am a bit of a dick as you've seen I've just
acted like a dick but at least I'm aware that I've acted like a
dick which makes me, you know: a bit less of a dick.'

Steph   Right.

Lewis   So what have you been doing? You and Waldorf?

Silence.

Lewis   . . . oh. Really? That?

Steph   Yeah.

Lewis   You've been . . . ?

Steph   Yeah.

Lewis   Having . . . ?

Steph   Yeah.

Lewis   . . . where? . . . here?

Steph   Yeah.

Lewis   In here?

Steph   Might have, yeah.

Lewis   Right. On the . . . our bed?

Steph   If that's your bed then yeah.

Lewis   It is.

Steph   Well then we did then yeah.

Lewis   OK.

Steph   Is that a bit like weird?

Lewis   No, it's . . . fine. You know, fill your boots. And your erm . . .

Steph   Can I have my joint back please?

Lewis   Yeah. Go for it.

Silence.

Lewis   So . . .

Steph   Yeah.

Lewis   That has gone right to my erm . . .

Steph   You're not very happy about this whole like bed thing, are you? I can tell.

Lewis   Not really but having smoked that I'm finding it sort of funny so I suppose it is funny then, if you just, find it funny?

Steph   Yeah.

Lewis   Was it . . . nice?

Steph   What?

Lewis   All the . . . ?

Steph   It was . . . OK.

Lewis   And was Waldorf . . . nice, at . . . ?

Steph   Yeah.

Lewis   You gonna go out with him?

Steph   Only met him today.

Lewis   Didn't stop you from . . .

Steph   Yeah but that's just coz he's like . . .

Lewis   What?

Steph   Easy.

Lewis   Obviously.

Steph   No, he's like, you know. Chilled out. I only really do that all that with people who are just gonna be totally like relaxed about it. No offence.

Lewis   Right. So are you saying that I'm not?

Steph   I dunno.

Lewis   Well you just did.

Steph   Didn't.

Lewis   So you don't think that, about me?

Steph   Erm . . .

Lewis   What?

Steph   Do you want me to be like, honest?

Lewis   Yeah.

Steph   Really?

Lewis   Yeah.

Steph   OK. Well. Every time we mention sex or something like that your legs sort of tense up.

Lewis   No they don't.

Steph   Yeah.

Lewis   Fuck off.

Steph   Breasts.

Lewis   . . . shit. Alright. Don't do that again. Please.

Steph   OK.

Lewis   Look, I'm just a bit fucked and stressed. Normally, I've got a very healthy . . . attitude, towards . . .

Steph   Sex?

Lewis   Yeah.

Steph   OK.

Lewis   I have. I'm really totally fucking completely fucking relaxed about it.

Steph   OK.

Lewis   *I am*.

Steph   I'm glad that you think that.

Lewis   Say that I am though.

Steph   What?

Lewis   Say that that I am say that I'm very relaxed about it.

Steph   Are you gonna force me to say that you are because I don't think that really suggests you. Like. Are.

Lewis   Point yeah point taken yeah. Sorry.

Steph   Alright.

Lewis   No, I'm really sorry, my head's gone. That's fucking strong.

Steph   OK.

Lewis   You know this is just with you – now – I am usually very . . .

Steph   Relaxed?

Lewis   Yeah.

Steph   Right.

Lewis   Before I settled down – married – I was really quite . . .

Steph   What?

Lewis   . . . raucous.

Steph   Yeah?

Lewis   Yeah. At Uni – girl-wise – used to match Waldorf, pound for . . . pound.

Steph   OK.

Lewis   In a nice way though like you say just cool nice casual stuff with nice people just doing what they want, when they want. Funky. Fresh. Dynamic (?). Is that even, vaguely believable?

Steph   Maybe, yeah.

Lewis   Yeah, I mean you've just caught me in a bad . . .

Steph   It's OK.

Lewis   . . . pickle. But it's difficult once it gets like this this sort of atmosphere to save it, doesn't it? To make it less . . . tense. Or weird.

Steph   It doesn't matter, Lewis.

Lewis   No, it feels like it does though. Steph. You know?

Pause.

Waldorf *enters.*

Waldorf   You having a moment?

Lewis   No. We were just. Talking.

Steph   Yeah.

Waldorf   What about? (Though before we start either of you wanna a whisky? Got some single malt. Laphroaig. Gorgeous. Fucking expensive. Tastes like the milk of the very fucking Gods. Stole it.)

Lewis   (OK.)

Steph   (Yeah, alright.)

Waldorf   (Cool.) So where were we?

Lewis   Erm. Yeah, we were just talking.

Waldorf   What about?

Steph   Lewis was saying he used to be a bit of a player.

Waldorf   'Hefty bollocks!'

Lewis   No I didn't, I didn't say it quite like that.

Steph   You did.

Lewis   No, well what I was saying all I was saying was that, that, that . . .

Waldorf   You have a speech impediment?

Lewis   No, I was saying, that, you know, I'm relaxed about . . . penetration. Of. People.

Waldorf   Right.

Lewis   You know?

Waldorf   No.

Steph   (Your legs just.)

Lewis   (No they didn't.)

Steph   (They did.)

Lewis   (Look, just shut up, alright?)

Waldorf   What's wrong with his legs?

Lewis   Nothing, my legs are brilliant. We were just saying that I've got a relaxed attitude to . . . physical love. That's all.

Waldorf   And yeah that's hefty bollocks.

Lewis   Why is it hefty bollocks?

Waldorf   Because it's not true mate.

Lewis   Course it is.

Waldorf   No.

Lewis   Why am I being attacked, here?

Waldorf   You're not.

Steph   You're really like, totally not.

Waldorf   No, we're just stating facts, calmly. Like Nuremberg.

Lewis   Well maybe I – as a Nazi, thank you – feel that you two are not currently the best placed people to judge me and what I am and what the facts of it . . . am. You know?

Waldorf   No yeah, you're probably right.

Lewis   Yeah?

Waldorf   Yeah. I mean: I'm me. And all that entails. And she's a fucking porn star for fuck's sake.

Lewis   What?

Waldorf   Yeah, so we're operating on totally different fucking levels to you. We're Champions League, you're Vauxhall Conference, or whatever it is now.

Lewis   Porn star?

Steph   Not, star.

Lewis   But, porn?

Steph   Sort of, yeah.

Lewis   You did, porn?

Steph   Not really. But, yeah, I did yeah.

Lewis   What did you do, on the . . . porn?

Steph   It wasn't like that.

Waldorf   No. It wasn't. Not really.

Lewis   What was it like?

Waldorf   Go on, tell him.

Steph   Yeah, it wasn't horrible commercial shit or anything like that.

Lewis   Yeah but what was it?

Steph   Well, there's this like festival. Called like: Humpfest.

Lewis   Humpfest?

Steph   Yeah. As in like: hump. And: fest. Started in America. Then came here.

Lewis   Yeah, and what is it?

Steph   I'm telling you. Like. Now.

Lewis   Alright.

Steph   It's like an alternative, like inclusive, like diversive, sexual festival.

Waldorf   Sounds fucking brilliant.

Steph   Yeah it is and it's really like artistic and expressive and they get loads of like totally different people to submit like bespoke, holistic like amateur porn that's different to all the sort of nasty like mainstream commercial stuff. It's not vanilla or anything like that there's still like anal and . . .

Waldorf Yeah?

Steph . . . yeah and group and watersports and stuff like that but it's not so sort of like fake tit, tan and teeth fifty cocks in like one girl bukkake ATM sort of thing.

Lewis OK.

Waldorf (Is that sort of porn bad then, is it?)

Steph (Sometimes, yeah.)

Lewis And then what happens?

Steph Yeah then you go to this like big like tent – the fest, the Humpfest – in the country near Suffolk or somewhere and you watch all the best tapes – like once – and then burn them all in like a big fire. Like a ritual. Cleansing. And also so it won't end up on like Youporn and make money for like corporations and Haliburton.

Lewis OK. Cool.

Steph Yeah, and it's good because you watch them together on this big screen with all the people who are like in them so no one's embarrassed or anything. Like, all in it together. Sort of thing.

Waldorf Austerity wank.

Steph I dunno.

Lewis And what, you did one?

Steph Last year, yeah. We came third. In our category.

Lewis Did you?

Steph Yeah.

Lewis What category?

Steph Two girls, one guy.

Lewis Really?

Steph Yeah.

Lewis Fuck.

Waldorf I told you.

Steph Not doing it this year but I've got some friends who are. Deadline's in like a few weeks.

Lewis Wow.

Steph Yeah. So you could like do that, couldn't you?

Lewis What?

Steph If you like, wanted to.

Lewis What?

Steph I'm just saying if you like wanted to prove how like un-Govey . . .

Lewis Relaxed?

Steph Yeah – legs – you could do that.

Lewis OK. But . . . well I'm in a relationship, so that's not really on the agenda. Sorry.

Waldorf You could do one with Morgan though.

Lewis What?

Steph That is a category. Couples.

Lewis Is it? OK. Interesting. Cool. Well I'll think about it.

Waldorf Will you?

Lewis Yeah.

Waldorf Fuck off.

Lewis What?

Waldorf I said fuck off.

Lewis Why?

Waldorf So hang on what, you're saying you're gonna plough your wife up in a porn film and then . . .

Steph   I think it's really more sort of like art, than porn.

Waldorf   OK, yeah – thank you Steph – so you're gonna respectfully do your spouse on an . . . an art film.

Steph   Yeah.

Waldorf   Yeah, and then watch it with a load of fucking sexual mambas in the countryside?

Lewis   I might.

Waldorf   You and your lovely lovely wife, are gonna do that? The one I met?

Lewis   Yeah. Who else am I gonna do it with?

Scene Three

Lewis *and* **Waldorf**.

Lewis   Morning, sailor.

Waldorf   Yeah, morning, Jesus.

Lewis   You alright?

Waldorf   Not really.

Lewis   My throat's gone.

Waldorf   My knees are, did we dance we danced didn't we?

Lewis   Yeah. That fucking club. 'Legends'.

Waldorf   Got it. Yep.

Lewis   Why did we go there?

Waldorf   Coz Steph knew the doorwoman. Intimately.

Lewis   God, she gets about, doesn't she?

Waldorf   'We all get about, Marjory.'

Lewis   Yeah. You want some water?

Waldorf   If you don't mind.

Lewis   Yeah, I'll just.

Waldorf   Where's wifey?

Lewis   Work.

Waldorf   Don't you have to er . . . ?

Lewis   What?

Waldorf   Work.

Lewis   Yeah, but I can do everything from home; I've called in. Data entry processing shit, so it's easy enough. Just need the laptop. Wireless. Radio Two. Corner yoghurt. Coke Zero. Away.

Waldorf   Abba. There was a lot of fucking Abba last night.

Lewis   There was. Most of which, we requested, I think.

Waldorf   Fuuuuck.

Lewis   Yeah.

Waldorf   You got any anise?

Lewis   What's that?

Waldorf   Anise, you know. The herb.

Lewis   Is it like aniseed?

Waldorf   Yeah, it is that yeah.

Lewis   No. Why?

Waldorf   This'll have to do then.

Lewis   What are you . . . ?

Waldorf   Picked up it in Georgia. Hangover cure. It's better with anise but still works.

Lewis   What does?

Waldorf Get some sugar. Whole tablespoon. Like that.
Place it under your tongue. Like that. Let it dissolve. Gives
you a bit o' pep.

Lewis Really?

Waldorf Yep.

Lewis Let's try it. (*Pause.*) Ooh. Yeah. Good tip.

Waldorf Now swallow.

Lewis OK. That's actually, really . . . helped.

Waldorf Georgians know about drinking, if anything.

Lewis '*Do they, Marjory?*'

Waldorf '*Of course, Jonathan, they're bloody Georgians!*'

Lewis The amount of shit you must know now.

Waldorf I dunno.

Lewis Yeah you must have done some pretty crazy shit out
there. In the yonder.

Waldorf I did a bit, yeah.

Lewis You probably told me all about it last night, my
memory's gone a bit . . .

Waldorf No, we didn't really talk about travelling, so
much, last night.

Lewis No?

Waldorf No.

Lewis What?

Waldorf I'm going to have to mention it first am I?

Lewis What?

Waldorf It.

Lewis What do you mean?

Waldorf 'The Proposed. Endeavour.'

Lewis Oh. That. No, I'll, I'll mention it.

Waldorf It is a bit of an elephant in the . . .

Lewis It's not an elephant in the . . .

Waldorf It is. I can hear it. Breathing.

Lewis No, I just hadn't talked about it yet. Thought you might wanna talk about, you know, other . . . things.

Waldorf Well yeah I can. If you want.

Lewis Coz I'll talk about it, yeah. Absolutely. Why not?

Waldorf You remember booking the hotel then?

Lewis What?

Waldorf The hotel. That you booked.

Lewis Er . . . Yeah. I do, yeah.

Waldorf The Royal.

Lewis Yes.

Waldorf Four star.

Lewis I remember that, yes.

Waldorf For tomorrow night.

Lewis How would I not remember that?

Waldorf Obviously. Just checking.

Lewis Well checked.

Waldorf Thank you.

Lewis Good . . . check . . .

Waldorf Yeah.

Lewis . . . mate.

Waldorf Yeah. But it's OK, you know, I'm not gonna make you do it, or anything.

Lewis What?

Waldorf I'm not gonna make you fuck me, am I?

Lewis Didn't say you were.

Waldorf Cool, so yeah, maybe you and Morgan can have the room, treat her to a night out or summat nice like that.

Lewis What?

Waldorf I dunno. I've never had a girlfriend for more than two months mate, let alone a fucking. Wife. You're the expert.

Lewis Hold on. What do you mean, make me fuck you?

Waldorf I just, you know. We agreed to do it, both a bit fucked up. Seemed really funny at the time. You booked a room. Trying to impress Steph probably with how progressive and Casanovafuck you are, I dunno. Fair enough. That's your game, play away sir, play away. So, you know, it's totally fine for you to back out.

Lewis It's OK for me to back out?

Waldorf Yeah.

Lewis Why do you think that I'm backing out?

Waldorf Because . . . it's you, Lewis.

Lewis And what does that mean?

Waldorf You're you.

Lewis Yes.

Waldorf And I'm. Me.

Lewis Yeah (?).

Waldorf Which means, that you are very much you. And I am I. And never the twain shall . . . be the same.

Lewis What?

Waldorf We're different, Lewis.

Lewis Are we?

Waldorf Yeah.

Lewis How?

Waldorf *Let me name the fucking . . .*

Lewis OK. Come on.

Waldorf Alright, alright. Firstly, you have a foreskin.

Lewis So?

Waldorf Which makes you naturally more inhibited.

Lewis It really fucking doesn't mate.

Waldorf Secondly, you're basically pretty much a Victorian when it comes to the sexual bearpit.

Lewis And what are you, a Jacobite?

Waldorf Yeah. Thirdly, how many women have you slept with?

Lewis That is the opposite of relevant to this.

Waldorf No, it isn't. How many?

Lewis You know how many. Well you can probably guess.

Waldorf Yeah. But I want you to say it.

Lewis No.

Waldorf Lewis.

Lewis . . . OK, erm . . .

Waldorf . . . ?

Lewis . . . two.

Waldorf Beth and Morgan, yeah?

Lewis   Yeah.

Waldorf   Despite all that shit you were coming out with last night about being a hot potato and cheese with minge at Uni. And then, we ask, how many women have I slept with?

Lewis   I don't know.

Waldorf   Guess. Go on.

Lewis   One.

Waldorf   Guess properly.

Lewis   Eight.

Waldorf   I slept with eight women in fucking Freshers' Week!

Lewis   Yeah, I wasn't taking notes.

Waldorf   You pretty much were. Come on. Guess properly.

Lewis   Alright. Forty? Fifty?

Waldorf   Higher.

Lewis   Sixty-five billion.

Waldorf   Lower.

Lewis   Sixty-three billion.

Waldorf   Seventy-one.

Lewis   Billion?

Waldorf   No. Women.

Lewis   OK.

Waldorf   One more – right? – and that's Islamic.

Lewis   OK. So?

Waldorf   So, I have slept with thirty-five-and-a-half times as many women as you have.

Lewis   So what?

Waldorf   So that says something, about us.

Lewis   Like what?

Waldorf   That we're different.

Lewis   Yeah, and how does that relate to . . . ?

Waldorf   It says that I would go through with this and that you wouldn't.

Lewis   No, not nece . . .

Waldorf   That I would turn up at the hotel room and you'd be at home, watching fucking 'Downton' with your lovely fragrant wife.

Lewis   Firstly, 'Downton' is on a Sunday, when it's on. Secondly, we haven't got a TV licence that's just for DVDs and iPlayer stuff. Thirdly, how fucking dare you?

Waldorf   Because it's true.

Lewis   It isn't. I'm just as likely to want to fuck you, as you are to want to fuck me.

Waldorf   You're just not, mate. This isn't worth arguing about. It's like Climate Change, you just have to accept it and move away from the fucking coast!

Lewis   No, I don't.

Waldorf   It's OK, honestly, you don't have to do it. I'm . . . absolving you.

Lewis   Well I – formally – do not accept your fucking . . . absolving!

Waldorf   There's no need to be so defensive about it.

Lewis   Yes there is: you're attacking me.

Waldorf   Calm down, alright?

Lewis   No, you're being a really really fucking patronising needless fucking cunt about this.

Waldorf   Am I?

Lewis   Yeah.

Waldorf   Well you're being a whiny little dickbag about it, so what?

Lewis   No I'm not.

Waldorf   Yes, yes you are. (*Pause.*) (We might be arguing a bit because of the sugar. You can crash a bit. After the initial . . .)

Lewis   No, we're arguing because you're making assumptions about me and my . . .

Waldorf   No, I'm just using the available evidence.

Lewis   *Hitler was just using the available evidence!*

Waldorf   (He really wasn't mate.)

Lewis   (No.)

Waldorf   OK. Well I didn't mean to upset you. As I say, I am just using the available evidence. Of your whole life.

Lewis   I'm serious. Stop it.

Waldorf   No.

Lewis   I will punch you.

Waldorf   No you won't.

Lewis   I will.

Waldorf   Go on then.

Lewis   OK.

Waldorf   Bring it.

Lewis   I will. I am. I will.

Waldorf   So where is it?

Lewis   Here.

Waldorf Yeah?

Lewis Yeah.

Silence.

Lewis Alright, I won't punch you. But I will, I will fuck you.

Waldorf OK, good.

Lewis Yeah?

Waldorf Yeah.

Lewis Right.

Waldorf Fine.

Lewis So we're no longer. Like. Arguing, are we?

Waldorf No.

Lewis Good.

Waldorf Yeah.

Lewis So let's do it then.

Waldorf Yeah, let's do it. Sorry, we're not being ironic now, are we? We're actually saying we're gonna do this, are we?

Lewis Yeah.

Waldorf OK. Why?

Lewis Because I'm not scared of it.

Waldorf Neither am I. But I'm also not scared of raping a starfish. Doesn't mean I'll do it. (Again.)

Lewis Well. Because . . .

Waldorf Because what?

Lewis You know, it's art, isn't it? Like Steph said, like we were saying all last night. For ages.

Waldorf Is it?

Lewis　Yeah, you know. We could be you know sort of
reclaiming . . . pornography. As a communal . . . art form
like we said. And that's a good thing to do, isn't it?

Waldorf　Is it?

Lewis　Yeah.

Waldorf　Why?

Lewis　Well. Honestly, do you not sometimes watch porn
and think: 'God, this is actually just horrible. He's horrible,
she's horrible. This is just a bit nasty and evil and sordid and
why am I on my own doing this?'

Waldorf　Yeah but I just wank through it.

Lewis　Yeah, so do I, you have to. But occasionally, you
watch something – porn, amateur stuff – where you see like
real life, actual warmth between people with stretch marks
and body fat and it's filthy and all that stuff but really it's just
two people – or three, or four – just really . . . you know?

Waldorf　What?

Lewis　I don't know. Sharing something. Genuinely like . . .
Joy. Love.

Waldorf　OK.

Lewis　And I think we'd all – secretly – deep down, like
to be able to fuck like that and then for people to watch us
and not be ashamed of it. Any of us. For it all to be out there,
for once.

Waldorf　OK (?).

Lewis　And yeah maybe, maybe you're right. I haven't slept
with that many people. I haven't gone out there and . . .

Waldorf　That doesn't mean . . .

Lewis　No, let me finish.

Waldorf　OK.

Lewis So this would be different. It wouldn't be cheating because you're not a woman and I don't fancy you. But still we could find that . . . warmth, maybe. On film. Capture it. For a moment. And then share it, with people. Without it ending up on Youjizz.com. Or Redtube. Or Spankwire. Or, any of them.

Pause.

Waldorf I think I know what you mean.

Lewis Yeah?

Waldorf Just about, yeah.

Lewis Have you ever done anything . . . with a guy?

Waldorf No. You?

Lewis No.

Waldorf (No. Obviously not.)

Lewis Though . . .

Waldorf What?

Lewis . . . well, you know I got to Uni early? Second year?

Waldorf Yeah.

Lewis When they let me stay in halls for the summer, coz of all that shit with my brother?

Waldorf Yeah.

Lewis And you remember Blockbuster? Up by the halls?

Waldorf Yeah.

Lewis Well, I found myself going in there, quite a lot. Just to get DVDs, Pringles, whatever. Popcorn. And one day.

Waldorf Yeah?

Lewis (One day.) Yeah. Guy behind the counter, out of nowhere, pretty much, recommended this documentary series to me about Isambard Kingdom Brunel and other great British, builders, engineers.

Waldorf   Great British builders and engineers?

Lewis   Yeah.

Waldorf   OK.

Lewis   Yeah. And they came in individual DVDs that you could rent. So, on his recommendation, I took out the first. And it was mainly about bridges. And it was mainly total fucking shit. But I bought it back in the next day. And he asked me what I thought. And I said: 'Yeah, it was wonderful, thank you, can I have the next one please?'

Waldorf   OK.

Lewis   And every day for about two weeks, I would come back in and say how great the next DVD in the series had been. And that meant I had to watch all of them – hours of it, fucking days of it – because he'd ask me all these questions about them and I wanted to be . . . enthusiastic and knowledgeable and . . . fluent. For him. Talking to him was, somehow . . .

Waldorf   OK.

Lewis   And a few nights in those weeks . . . I did think . . .

Waldorf   What?

Lewis   . . . about his forearms.

Waldorf   OK.

Lewis   Which were quite. Defined.

Waldorf   OK.

Lewis   And his shoulders. Quite a broad guy.

Waldorf   OK.

Lewis   And then I thought about . . . about kissing him.

Waldorf   Good.

Lewis   Which I . . . yeah, I liked.

Waldorf   Top.

Lewis   Yeah. But when I thought – just thought – about doing any more. In my head, his balls and his arse would sort of swing into view and ruin it all.

Waldorf   They would, yeah.

Lewis   Yeah. I don't even know if he was gay, or not, or anything.

Waldorf   How did you leave it?

Lewis   With the final DVD. About the UK's largest free-standing chimneys. I couldn't bring myself to go back in. Say goodbye. So I just put it through the little letterbox at the front, ran off.

Waldorf   You ever go back?

Lewis   No.

Waldorf   Why not? (*Pause.*) You big fat bender.

Lewis   Yeah. Maybe I shouldn't have told you that.

Waldorf   No, you should. You should.

Lewis   Yeah?

Waldorf   Yeah.

Lewis   So, you know, don't try and . . . limit me.

Waldorf   OK, I won't mate.

Lewis   Thank you.

Silence.

Waldorf   Alright, so let's do it then.

Lewis   Yeah?

Waldorf   Yeah. I mean, maybe that's why I came back. To fuck you in the arse. And cum my manfat Waldorf spunkseed into your . . . brown dirty hole.

Lewis   Isn't it because you had nowhere else to go?

Waldorf   What?

Lewis   No, sorry that wasn't meant to sound quite as . . .

Waldorf   I could have gone, other places.

Lewis   Yeah.

Waldorf   I could have. I've been on my own for seven fucking years, I can cope with another . . .

Lewis   Yeah.

Waldorf   By now. Few more weeks of it.

Lewis   Yeah.

Waldorf   I had to.

Lewis   I know.

Waldorf   I just thought . . . I thought that you would want to see me, that's all. I thought that you would want to be the first person, to see me back.

Lewis   I did. I do. I am.

Waldorf   I thought that I'd be . . . welcome.

Lewis   You are.

Waldorf   (Here.) Yeah?

Lewis   Yeah. Of course.

Waldorf   Don't think Morgan likes me that much.

Lewis   Well you did stick your penis through the er and then drag me back pissed at half four in the morning, after leaving the flat in a total fucking state and not washing the bedsheets.

Waldorf   Yeah, we probably should have invited her out, shouldn't we?

Lewis   Yeah, I was going to. Text didn't send. Thought it had.

Waldorf   Yeah.

Silence.

Lewis   You alright?

Waldorf   Yeah, I just . . . You have so much time to think on that last plane home. Everything that's waiting for you. Or not.

Lewis   Yeah.

Waldorf   I mean, I've never finished . . . anything. Not properly. I always leave just before . . . So maybe yeah, let's finish this.

Lewis   . . . OK.

Waldorf   Small. Achievable. Goals.

Silence.

Waldorf   What will Morgan say? If you tell her?

Lewis   Not much.

Waldorf   Really?

Lewis   No, I don't think so.

Waldorf   I dunno, women can be pretty funny about that sort of stuff.

Lewis   Can they?

Waldorf   Yeah. A lot.

Lewis   Well Morgan won't be, she's not a normal woman. She's great.

Waldorf   You sure? I don't wanna break up a marriage, for a silly little bet.

Lewis Don't be stupid. I'll tell her tonight. Be fine. She's very . . . open-minded.

Waldorf Is she?

Lewis Yeah. Massively. Huge . . . mind.

Waldorf OK then.

Scene Four

Lewis *and* **Morgan**.

Morgan What's wrong? Power cut?

Lewis No.

Morgan Again? Fuck sake.

Lewis No, it's romantic.

Morgan Is it?

Lewis Yeah.

Morgan Oh fuck, you made dinner? Proper dinner? With like. Food. And. Plates?

Lewis Yeah.

Morgan Wow, that is a lot of candles.

Lewis I know, yeah. Took me ages.

Morgan Fuck of a lot.

Lewis You like?

Morgan Bit of a fire risk but, yeah. It'll be a pretty death.

Lewis Right.

Morgan Where's Wallypants?

Lewis I sorted him out with the Travel Lodge, finally.

Morgan OK. And what's all this for? Make up for last night?

Lewis   No. Just, because, you know, I love you, dude.

Morgan   Dude?

Lewis   Yeah, this is to make up for . . .

Morgan   Turning up at five in the morning like a pair of mental screaming bandits?

Lewis   Yeah.

Morgan   Right. So what's in it then?

Lewis   Erm, it's a new one. Fennel. Lamb. Bit o' chilli. Onion. White wine sauce. Boo-ya.

Morgan   Fuck.

Lewis   Yeah, fuck is right, madam.

Morgan   I'm impressed.

Lewis   Yeah?

Morgan   Yeah.

Lewis   'Wine, guvnor?'

Morgan   'Go on my son.'

Silence.

Morgan   So is Waldorf alright?

Lewis   Yeah.

Morgan   He's a one. Slash, card.

Lewis   He is.

Morgan   Never seen you like that with a guy before.

Lewis   How do you mean?

Morgan   Do you not remember last night, what he did to you, after you came in?

Lewis   No, I don't. What?

Morgan   Well, you'd swapped shoes for some reason (?) while you were out and you'd done your laces up – his laces up – way too tight and you couldn't get them off, so he was like . . . on the floor, in front of you, on his knees, yanking your shoes off ya and sort of berating you for it in the process. Calling you all these names under his breath.

Lewis   Was he?

Morgan   Yeah. And it was like how my nan would talk to my granddad or something.

Lewis   Sorry.

Morgan   No. Just funny to watch. Sort of. Were you that close at Uni?

Lewis   For the first two years, yeah.

Morgan   Then what happened?

Lewis   Third year, he started going out more. You wouldn't see him for like weeks at a time. Then he dropped out.

Morgan   You've barely mentioned him.

Lewis   Yeah, I wasn't sure I'd ever see him again, to be honest. You'd get the odd e-mail from him but. He's not even on Facebook. He reckons it's controlled by the CIA.

Morgan   You're glad he's back then?

Lewis   Yeah.

Morgan   You alright?

Lewis   Yeah.

Morgan   Thanks though. For this.

Lewis   Alright.

Morgan   And you can soundproof walls, apparently. Guy at work told me. Lewis? You listening?

Lewis   Yeah.

Morgan   And it's not too expensive. He said he'd get us a quote, he's got a mate who . . .

Lewis   Right.

Morgan   Lewis.

Lewis   What?

Morgan   I'm talking.

Lewis   I know.

Morgan   Like. Words and shit.

Lewis   Yeah look, I need to er, tell you something.

Morgan   Are you pregnant? Fuck, is your mum coming down?

Lewis   No. But still you might. Spaz out, a bit.

Morgan   Why?

Lewis   Well me and Waldorf have agreed . . . to do something.

Morgan   What?

Lewis   Nothing much.

Morgan   Well come on stop being odd tell me.

Lewis   Yeah but you might. Freak.

Morgan   Stop saying that.

Lewis   Alright, yeah, well Waldorf has a . . . film-making. Opportunity. And I said that I'd help him out with it.

Morgan   For al-Qaeda?

Lewis   No.

Morgan   So why are you being all . . . ?

Lewis   Yeah, I just know that Waldorf and I didn't behave too well. Last night. And I was worried that you might be worried about me spending too much time with him. On this film.

Morgan   He's your best mate. Apparently. Just if you're gonna go out like that again, tell me. Or take me, you know?

Lewis   OK.

Morgan   So what's the film?

Lewis   Er yeah. It's experimental. Art.

Morgan   He doesn't seem very arty.

Lewis   No, he is, loves it.

Morgan   What's he gonna do with it?

Lewis   Act.

Morgan   And what are you gonna do?

Lewis   Help him. Act.

Morgan   Help him act?

Lewis   As much as I can, yeah.

Morgan   What does that mean?

Lewis   It's erm . . . Well it's a bit complicated. Technical.

Morgan   Alright, well who's making it? Like directing it, writing it?

Lewis   It's gonna be improvised, mainly.

Morgan   What, Mike Leigh sort of stuff?

Lewis   In a way, yeah.

Morgan   OK then.

Lewis   You don't mind?

Morgan   No. Why would I?

Lewis   Great. Top up?

Morgan   No.

Lewis   (And I might be in it, as well.)

Morgan   What?

Lewis   The film. I might be in it.

Morgan   Really?

Lewis   Yeah.

Morgan   Acting?

Lewis   Yeah.

Morgan   You?

Lewis   Yeah.

Morgan   You can't, though.

Lewis   I can. Probably. Anyway, I won't have many lines, I don't think.

Morgan   OK. So who's making it then? Students, or?

Lewis   It's gonna be self-financed. Waldorf's putting up some of the money for it, I think.

Morgan   And are you putting money in?

Lewis   I might. If you were happy with that?

Morgan   Depends how much.

Lewis   Well no, actually, no, don't worry about the money.

Morgan   OK. And what's the film about?

Lewis   Modern. Attitudes. Towards. Sex.

Morgan   OK. Does it have a story?

Lewis   Yeah, there'll be a general. Arc. Sort of.

Morgan   Sounds a bit vague.

Lewis   No it has a very specific end point. A climax (?).

Morgan   OK. And when's it filming?

Lewis   Tomorrow. Tomorrow night.

Morgan   He's only been back two days.

Lewis   Yeah, that's how he rolls. Quickly.

Morgan   Where will it be filmed?

Lewis   The Royal.

Morgan   Hotel?

Lewis   Yeah.

Morgan   Posh.

Lewis   No.

Morgan   Yeah. Dead expensive.

Lewis   . . . not really, no.

Morgan   It is.

Lewis   No, well they've only got like one room for like one night.

Morgan   Wait a minute.

Lewis   What?

Morgan   . . . Waldorf is filming a . . . a film, about attitudes to sex and it's going to be shot in a hotel room over one night?

Lewis   Yeah.

Morgan   Is it. Porn?

Lewis   No.

Morgan   So what is it?

Lewis   . . . art.

Morgan   Art?

Lewis   Yeah, it's an artistic examination of . . . porn.

Morgan   Is he gonna fuck anyone?

Lewis   . . . possibly. Yeah.

Morgan   Are you joking?

Lewis   No.

Morgan   And you're gonna be there?

Lewis   That's the plan, yeah.

Morgan   Wait a minute, who's he gonna fuck? A prostitute?

Lewis   No, the other person isn't a. No. 'Prostitute'. No.

Morgan   But it's an actress who'll be having sex on camera, with Waldorf, for money?

Lewis   The other person won't be paid, no.

Morgan   They're doing it, for free?

Lewis   Yeah.

Morgan   Why?

Lewis   Probably lots of complex socio-economic, cultural reasons.

Morgan   Right.

Lewis   So what do you think?

Morgan   I think it's fucking weird, Lewis.

Lewis   Yeah but he's a mate, you know?

Morgan   Are you gonna be watching him, having . . . ?

Lewis   I might have to watch, yeah. Unless I close my eyes, I suppose.

Morgan   But if you're acting in it, that doesn't mean you'll be . . . with this woman, as well?

Lewis   No, don't be stupid, no. Definitely not. No. That is not what is going to happen.

Morgan   So you're not asking me to let you have sex with another woman?

Lewis   No.

Morgan   No?

Lewis   No.

Morgan   This is still fucking weird though, Lewis. That hasn't changed.

Lewis   I know. I know. I'm sorry, I am.

Morgan   Is that why you made all this? Grand inferno?

Lewis   No. Yeah. No. I just want to help a mate out, that's all.

Morgan   Yeah, but how would you feel if I asked you if I could watch a mate of mine getting fucked by a stranger?

Lewis   I'd be fine, with that.

Morgan   Would you?

Lewis   Yeah.

Morgan   You wouldn't though, would ya?

Lewis   Yeah, I would. But as I said, I won't watch him. Do that. With a woman. I'll leave. If that happens. Promise.

Morgan   Can't someone else help him out?

Lewis   No, it has to be me. I mean, I'm all he's got now. He hasn't got any other friends, family. Literally. Just me, and that's it. You know?

Silence.

Morgan   OK then.

Lewis   Yeah?

Morgan   If you want to.

Lewis   I do, yeah. You don't mind?

Morgan   I do, but that doesn't seem to be enough for you not to want to do it, so I'm not gonna stop you, Lewis. Am I?

Pause.

Lewis   Where you going?

Morgan   To the DJ booth.

Music.

Lewis   Good . . .

Morgan *exits.*

Lewis   . . . luck. (Fuck.)

Pause.

Waldorf *enters.*

Lewis   What you doing?

Waldorf   Sorry, forgot something.

Lewis   Mate I told you to leave the key here. That's the only spare.

Waldorf   Oh yeah, sorry. Well have it now. Just wanted to get the Laphroaig in, it's so fucking expensive, seems a waste to leave it with you lot.

Lewis   Yeah, well take it and go then.

Waldorf   How did she . . . ?

Lewis   What?

Waldorf   . . . take it?

Lewis   Good, yeah. But honestly, you need to fuck off, before she . . .

Waldorf   Oh, is she in the . . . ?

Lewis   Yeah yeah, come on get the bottle, and fuck off.

Morgan *enters.*

Music off.

Morgan   Hello.

Waldorf   Hey.

Lewis   He just . . . forgot something. And he's taking it away now. Aren't you?

Waldorf   Yep.

Morgan   OK. Sorry Lewis, could you sort the fan out please?

Lewis   Now?

Morgan   Yeah definitely now, yeah.

Lewis   . . . oh, alright, yeah. OK. Good.

Lewis *exits.*

Pause.

Morgan   So you're making a film then?

Waldorf   Yeah.

Morgan   Exciting.

Waldorf   Yeah. Hopefully. 'Touch wood.' You know?

Morgan   Yeah. You're very . . . brave, I suppose.

Waldorf   Am I?

Morgan   Yeah. Most people wouldn't . . .

Waldorf   No. They wouldn't, would they?

Morgan   No. No.

Lewis *enters.*

Lewis   Everything . . . alright?

Waldorf   Yeah.

Morgan   We're just talking about the film that you're gonna . . .

Lewis   . . . oh. Right.

Waldorf   And you're cool with it?

Lewis   Yeah, she is, but we wanna have dinner now, so do you mind . . . ?

Waldorf   Yeah yeah yeah sorry I'll leave the lovetits to it.

Lewis   No worries.

Waldorf   And don't you worry, Morgan: I'll be gentle with him.

Morgan   What?

Lewis   Just fuck off, yeah?

Morgan   What you say?

Lewis   Please.

Waldorf   No, you know, it's OK, I'll break him in easy, à la Brokeback. Won't scare the horses. '*WE'VE GOT A BLEEDER IN ROOM 4!*'

Silence.

Morgan   What are you talking about?

Waldorf   You know, him and me . . .

Morgan   What?

Lewis   Mate.

Waldorf   . . . having the old . . . making, you know . . .

Morgan   No.

Waldorf   . . . love. With each other.

Morgan   What?

Waldorf   On the . . . film. The film that you were . . . just
. . . Or maybe you weren't erm . . . done with the er . . .
(Oh fuck.)

Lewis   Yeah.

Morgan   Yeah. I . . . Yeah.

Silence.

Waldorf   Well, I'll leave you to it then. Campers (?).

Lewis   If you would.

Waldorf   Bye . . . then.

Lewis   . . . bye.

Morgan   Yeah. Goodbye.

Waldorf *exits.*

Silence.

Morgan   What the holy fuck?

Lewis   Yeah that's just . . .

Morgan   What is this?

Lewis   A joke. Just a joke.

Morgan   It's not though, is it?

Lewis   . . . no.

Morgan   So what is it?

Lewis   Art.

Morgan   That's meaningless.

Lewis   I know, yeah.

Morgan   So what is it?

Lewis   Look. Look.

Morgan   I really fucking am, OK?

Lewis   Yeah. Just. Recently, I've just started to feel a bit . . .

Morgan   What?

Lewis   And it's not anyone's fault or anything but I have, I've started to feel somewhat . . .

Morgan   . . . ?

Lewis   . . . cramped. Here.

Morgan   Cramped?

Lewis   Yeah.

Morgan   And what does that mean?

Lewis   It means that I'm worried. About my life. That it's . . .

Morgan   What?

Lewis   . . . going. Away.

Morgan   And what does that mean?

Lewis   It means that. You know. Where's my life. Like. Going?

Morgan   To being a family. To maybe one day getting a house and . . .

Lewis   Yeah, but . . .

Morgan   What?

Lewis   There's more to it though, isn't there?

Morgan   Like what? Waldorf?

Lewis   No, listen.

Morgan   I am.

Lewis   . . . OK. (*Pause.*) Alright. Alright. I look at my dad, sometimes. And he's spent his whole life building up his business. Making sure that the business is OK. He's *always* been on trips and conferences and conventions and the rest of the time he was with us. There didn't seem to be anything that was just. *Him.*

Morgan   . . . OK.

Lewis   And I don't wanna end up like that.

Morgan   So what you want to fuck Waldorf, so you don't end up turning into your dad?

Lewis   Yeah. No, but . . . I don't know. I just think that, if I get something like this out of my system *now*, then that will probably help us, in the long run, you know? And it's not an orientation thing, or anything. A switcheroo. It's not, it's just. An experience thing. Because I'll be like: 'Yeah, well now, I've seen the world a bit. I've done things, tried things, I haven't just stayed at home and watched you going through your fucking e-mails every night and then having to turn on the fan for you every time you have a nasty fucking poo.'

Morgan   You poo too!

Lewis   Yes, exactly! That's exactly it though, isn't it?

Morgan   Is it?

Lewis   Yeah, no. Fuck. Erm . . . Look, you know that I . . . I totally, adore you, Morgan. I do. More than anything. You're my whole life. Every page of it, that matters, is you. But still, I'm quite . . . I am. And I didn't think that I was but . . . I am. I'm . . . (*Pause.*) Lost.

Morgan   And what, you think I'm . . . found?

Lewis   Yeah. That's exactly what's so great about you.

Morgan   Great?

Lewis   Yeah.

Morgan   That what, I don't look outside of us, for . . . ? That I don't have other . . . things I wanna do, or . . . ? That I like living like this . . . ? That what, I haven't given things up, for you?

Lewis   No, coz you're not . . . you're just . . . *you*, aren't you? *Solid*. There.

Morgan   Solid?

Lewis   Yeah.

Morgan   Like a: shelving unit?

Lewis   Yeah. Exactly. Yeah.

Silence.

Morgan   Do you know how many men that I could have . . . ? Whilst we've been . . . ?

Lewis   . . . no.

Morgan   . . . together. If I'd wanted, to what . . . experience something outside . . . of this. The numbers of guys that I could have just . . . But I haven't because I thought that we . . .

Lewis   Numbers?

Morgan   Yeah, numbers, yeah.

Lewis   . . . how many, numbers?

Morgan   Guess. Go on.

Lewis   I don't want to.

Morgan   No, you don't.

Lewis   OK. Well obviously I haven't framed this in the right . . .

Morgan   It's not how you frame it, Lewis. It's what you want to do. And it's how you see me, isn't it?

Lewis   Yeah but it's . . . it's just sounding bad as I'm saying it but it's all much better in my head, honestly.

Morgan   It would have to be.

Lewis   No, look you always fucking do this.

Morgan   What?

Lewis   Spin you spin me back what I'm saying to the point where I'm like . . .

Morgan   I'm not spinning anything. I'm just letting you talk.

Lewis   OK. (Fuck.)

Morgan   Yeah.

Silence.

Morgan   You really want to have sex with him?

Lewis   Not him, specifically.

Morgan   Just someone . . . what . . . ? Who isn't . . . me?

Silence.

Lewis   Yeah. Yes.

Morgan   OK.

Silence.

Morgan   Know how that feels.

Lewis   Right. What?

Morgan   Feeling like you need to – what – branch out, maybe?

Lewis   Cool. Yeah. Well we all do, sometimes. It's natural.

Morgan   Yeah. It is.

Lewis   What are you . . . ?

Silence.

Morgan   You remember when I went to visit Molly? About a year ago.

Lewis   Yeah.

Morgan   We went to this house party that some of her doctor mates were having in this mental sort of loft warehouse thing.

Lewis   Yeah. You said.

Morgan   Yeah. And um. I got really pissed. Out of it. And I was feeling . . . very . . . (*Pause.*) And I did . . . Some stuff. With a man. In a room. And it was. Great.

Lewis   . . . was it?

Morgan   Yeah. And in a way, you're right. It was good to come home, to you, after. Because I knew what I was coming back to. I knew you were what I wanted, really, probably more than I knew that before.

Lewis   OK.

Morgan   So yeah, maybe you're right, I dunno.

Lewis   It was great?

Morgan   Yeah.

Lewis   Wow. Wow. Um . . . OK. Alright. I suppose, I should be really fucking mad with you, now then, and playing all sorts of mad guilt shit?

Morgan   Yeah.

Lewis   Yeah. But I . . . I can't really, can I?

Morgan   No.

Lewis   No.

Pause.

Morgan   So yeah. Do it. Get it out of your . . . system. If you need that. Whatever, it is. Worked for me.

Lewis   Did it?

Morgan   Yeah.

Lewis   Great. That is . . . really, great.

Silence.

Lewis   Well I suppose I have to do it now, don't I?

Morgan   Yeah. I think you do. Yeah. (Fuck.)

Lewis   Yeah.

Part Two

Scene One

Lewis, *alone*.

Silence.

Waldorf *enters*.

Waldorf   Fuck.

Lewis   I know.

Waldorf   It's gorgeous. Good work.

Lewis   . . . yeah.

Waldorf   I mean it. God, you could film a proper actual porn thing here.

Lewis   Isn't that what we're doing?

Waldorf   No, you know. Lighting rigs. Roadies. Catering staff. Fluffers. Fifteen-year-old Romanian girls who just wanna go home and have a wash.

Lewis   Right.

Waldorf   All this space.

Lewis   Yeah.

Waldorf   Reminds me of Bangkok, a bit.

Lewis   How come?

Waldorf   You can get places like this there, dirt cheap: live it up.

Lewis   This wasn't.

Waldorf   What, cheap?

Lewis   No.

Waldorf   Fuck, the view.

Lewis   Yeah.

Waldorf   Lake. Gardens. So green, all of it.

Lewis   Twelve acres.

Waldorf   Can you afford this?

Lewis   No. Had to call Mum. Get a bridging loan.

Waldorf   '*Mother!*'

Lewis   Yeah.

Waldorf   What did you say it was for?

Lewis   What?

Waldorf   The money?

Lewis   Yeah, she's stopped asking me for reasons.

Waldorf   Good of her.

Lewis   Not really, she is calculating all the interest.

Waldorf   Fair enough.

Lewis   At quite high-end commercial rates.

Waldorf   Fucking, bankers (!).

Lewis   Yeah. She reckons it's for my own good. Probably right, bless her.

Waldorf   Yeah. Fucking . . . mothers.

Lewis   You ever hear from yours?

Waldorf   . . . no.

Lewis   Do you know where she is?

Waldorf   No. Could probably find out, if I wanted but . . .

Lewis   Is she still . . . ?

Waldorf   Yeah. From what I hear. Worse, these days, I think.

Lewis   Right. Sorry.

Waldorf   No, you know. 'Man hands on misery to man.'

Lewis   Yeah. What's that from?

Waldorf   (Dunno, something: old.) I could chip in though, you know? For this.

Lewis   It's paid for now.

Waldorf   Dunt matter, I can still . . .

Lewis   Have you got any money?

Waldorf   No but I could get some. Shift a bit of Ket, or my arsehole.

Lewis   No, anyway, I called them. My fault.

Waldorf   I did sort of wind you up as you were doing it.

Lewis   Knew what I was doing.

Waldorf   Yeah, you did. What's the shitter like?

Lewis   Like a sultan's.

Waldorf   Yeah?

Lewis   Have a look.

Waldorf *exits*.

Waldorf (*off*)   Holy tittyfuck!

Lewis   Yeah, I had the first properly quiet poo in there, that I've had in months. It was exquisite.

Waldorf (*off*)   Yeah?

Lewis   Yeah.

Waldorf (*off*)   You had a shower though, after?

Lewis   Yeah. Have you?

Waldorf (*off*)   What?

Lewis   Showered?

Waldorf enters.

Waldorf   Yeah, should have done it here though. You alright?

Lewis   Yeah, I'm just . . .

Waldorf   What?

Lewis   This is just . . .

Waldorf   Lewis? You OK?

Lewis   . . . sort of place I'd like to bring up a kid, you know? Not in a hotel, obviously, but on the edge of the country. Nature. Deer. Men in hats, with sticks.

Waldorf   Have you been . . . ?

Lewis   No.

Waldorf   Crying?

Lewis   No. Went for a walk, just now. Took in the grounds.

Waldorf   Do you want a hug mate?

Lewis   No.

Silence.

Waldorf   I bought a fuckload o' lube. I didn't know which type was best, so I just got 'em all in. There's erm yeah: 'Woohoo! Water Based Intimate Organic Lubricant'; 'Durex Sensilube'; 'Slide & Ride' (?); 'Golden Girl Anal Jelly'; 'WET Pheromone Lubricant, 100ml'.

Lewis   Impressive.

Waldorf   It was a bit of a panic buy, really. I didn't want to spend any longer in the shop reading all the fucking. Descriptions.

Lewis   Yeah.

Waldorf   I was getting quite the looks.

Lewis   I bet.

Waldorf   'Golden Girl Anal Jelly is a specially formulated anal lube, designed to deliver low-friction fun (!). Whether you're inserting a thumb, a hammer, a foot – or all three – there's no sweeter way to penetrate . . . Lewis.' Nice. Personal. No?

Lewis   No.

Waldorf   Fuck, are you sure that you're . . . ?

Lewis   Yeah I'm OK yeah.

Waldorf   Yeah?

Lewis   Defo.

Waldorf   Alright. We could go for another walk maybe, get some fresh air?

Lewis   I don't want to.

Waldorf   OK. But to be honest mate, this isn't really like . . . helping, you know?

Lewis   What?

Waldorf   You being all . . .

Lewis   I know.

Waldorf   Not very sexy cowboy.

Lewis   No.

Waldorf   *'Doesn't make me stiff Jonathan!'*

Lewis   No.

Waldorf   *'Or wet Marjory!'*

Lewis   Jesus.

Waldorf   Yeah.

Lewis   Jesus.

Waldorf   Yeah. Maybe have some water or a, a lie down maybe?

Lewis   OK.

Waldorf   I've got a bottle of gin in me bag if that'll help? Though I didn't get any mixers. Mini bar?

Lewis   No, we can't afford it. At all. Alright?

Waldorf   OK. We should just relax though. Put some music on, maybe?

Lewis   Did you have a haircut?

Waldorf   . . . yeah.

Lewis   For this?

Waldorf   . . . for the camera, yeah. Not for you. (Bighead.)

Lewis   Right.

Waldorf   This woman did it.

Lewis   Makes you look younger.

Waldorf   Does it?

Lewis   Yeah.

Waldorf   I told her I was going to a birthday party, for some reason (?).

Lewis   Yeah?

Waldorf   Yeah, and I got into this whole fucking like, extended backstory.

Lewis   Like what?

Waldorf   That I'd been working on an oilrig. Over the summer. In the Atlantic. With a load of Poles (?). And I said it was the birthday was of a guy – a fellow . . . whatever . . .

oilrigman? – Felix (?), who'd had both his legs and all his fingers – and his ears, and his lips – blown off by an exploding, massive oil pipe.

Lewis Right.

Waldorf Explained my nerves a bit, you know?

Lewis Yeah.

Waldorf I said I was worried about how best to shake his hand and maintain both our respective dignities.

Lewis Right.

Waldorf What was left of his hands, you know.

Lewis Yeah.

Waldorf Stumps.

Lewis Yeah.

Waldorf *'I'm stumped!'*

Lewis Yeah.

Waldorf She was very understanding, actually.

Lewis Was she?

Waldorf Yeah, gave me the number of a counsellor, who'd helped her out when she started having panic attacks, in crowded spaces. Lovely woman, really. Though pretty fucking gullible. And she can't cut hair for shit.

Lewis I dunno. Suits you.

Waldorf Does it?

Lewis Gives you a fifties sort of a look.

Waldorf OK. You sure you don't want a hug?

Lewis Yeah, I'm OK yeah.

Waldorf Where's the camera?

Lewis   Down there.

Waldorf   Cool, looks alright. 'Sony HDRCX116EB High Definition Handycam Camcorder. Black.'

Lewis   Yeah.

Waldorf   So we can hold it in our hands and stuff whilst we . . . ?

Lewis   Yeah. Or just put it on the side.

Waldorf   If I do that, is it on then?

Lewis   Yeah, if the light is.

Waldorf   Like that?

Lewis   Yeah.

Waldorf   Wow. We should do an intro.

Lewis   What?

Waldorf   You know, introduce ourselves. To the crowd.

Lewis   OK. Like. Now?

Waldorf   Yeah, when else?

Lewis   . . . OK.

Waldorf   Alright. So this is, I'm Waldorf. And this is Lewis. 'Hello!'

Lewis   Hey.

Waldorf   We are going to be your entertainment for the evening. We hope. Lewis?

Lewis   Yeah, we hope you . . . what? Enjoy . . . this?

Waldorf   (Yeah, maybe with a bit less dread mate.)

Lewis   I hope that you . . . enjoy it.

Waldorf   (Me or them?)

Lewis   Either. Both.

Waldorf   Yeah?

Lewis   . . . yeah.

Waldorf   Seriously.

Lewis   What?

Waldorf   You have to I think you have to buck the fucking Uncle fucking Buckfuck up here mate.

Lewis   I'm sorry.

Waldorf   For them, if not for me.

Lewis   Yeah.

Waldorf   Think of your audience.

Lewis   OK.

Waldorf   Fucking hell, I've never seen anyone so depressed by fucking deer (!).

Lewis   OK.

Waldorf   Just, you know: *cheer up*.

Lewis   OK.

Waldorf   I mean it.

Lewis   I am. I will.

Waldorf   Now.

Lewis   Alright.

Waldorf   There we go. Little smile, for me. Now, one for the camera. And say: hello you dirty fuckers.

Lewis   Hello you dirty fuckers (?).

Waldorf   Yeah, at least you tried, alright? So what now?

Lewis   I suppose we start all the . . . business.

Waldorf   Yeah. And on the whole lube thing. We haven't really talked about which way round we're gonna . . .

Lewis   Do . . . ?

Waldorf   Yeah. Do. Who do . . . who. Who will do who.
Have we? Not, seriously.

Lewis   No.

Waldorf   But I've got a suggestion.

Lewis   Please.

Waldorf   Well, whoever's got the biggest . . . should like
take the other one, yeah? That way it's sort o' natural justice,
isn't it, for having a bigger knob? And it will be kinder. To
the environment. More sustainable, if you know what I
mean.

Lewis   Waldorf.

Waldorf   What? Yeah, have I gone right face in to the big
old nittyfuckinggritty too soon for ya?

Lewis   Yeah maybe yeah.

Waldorf   Alright. Well OK then, let's start – hang back a bit,
ninja – with the basics, maybe? And then. You know: build
up. To that. So yeah, maybe we should just start to get
undressed and stuff, first?

Lewis   You think?

Waldorf   Yeah, or actually maybe we should get undressed
as we do it? Sort of undress each other, in the moment.

Lewis   Difficult to plan out like that though, isn't it?

Waldorf   Maybe. Maybe it isn't.

Lewis   Yeah but maybe it is.

Waldorf   Alright.

Lewis   And what about erm . . . ?

Waldorf   What?

Lewis   . . . stiffies?

Waldorf   What about 'em?

Lewis   How are we gonna like . . . get them?

Waldorf   By . . .

Lewis   What?

Waldorf   . . . I thought we would, you know, stimulate, each other. That is: traditional.

Lewis   Really?

Waldorf   Yeah. How else are we gonna do it? An erection dance? A Haka?

Lewis   No, I just thought we might watch some porn – straight porn – first.

Waldorf   Together?

Lewis   Yeah.

Waldorf   And what. Wank off? In a little row?

Lewis   Ideally, yeah.

Waldorf   OK.

Lewis   Is that a bit weird?

Waldorf   A little bit.

Lewis   Sorry.

Waldorf   No, stop being all fucking . . . pathetic, about it. We're here to fuck.

Lewis   OK.

Waldorf   I mean it. Man up.

Lewis   Alright. Yeah.

Waldorf   Good. So have you got any then?

Lewis   What?

Waldorf   Porn? DVDs or something, or maybe there's an in-house adult channel thingy on the?

Lewis   No, I haven't got any . . . we can just use our phones. Cheaper.

Waldorf   Can't use mine.

Lewis   Why not?

Waldorf   It's a Nokia brick. Unless you wanna whack off to Snake?

Lewis   Well we can use mine. Access some streaming sites, I'm on the wi-fi.

Waldorf   No, the screen's too small.

Lewis   Still works.

Waldorf   Really?

Lewis   Yeah, you can still see all that's . . . happening, on it.

Waldorf   You wank off to your phone?

Lewis   It's what people do now.

Waldorf   No, they use computers, don't they? I do.

Lewis   Yeah but me and Morgan share the laptop and however much you delete the history, I just don't trust cookies and cache files and pop-ups and . . .

Waldorf   Oh right, fair enough.

Lewis   If she saw my history.

Waldorf   Yeah.

Lewis   Reads like a list of very specific, low-level war crimes.

Waldorf   Yeah. Never done it to a phone before.

Lewis   It works fine.

Waldorf   With two of us, though?

Lewis   Just have to position ourselves right.

Waldorf   Yeah. But honestly mate, it feels a bit like.
Cheating.

Lewis   OK.

Waldorf   You know because I thought we would just . . .
organically . . .

Lewis   Organically?

Waldorf   Organically, sort of, you know. Emerge.

Lewis   Emerge?

Waldorf   Yeah.

Lewis   Right.

Waldorf   And also, just to say, once I start going, I really
like to, you know: finish.

Lewis   Do you?

Waldorf   I'm like a juggernaut, in that respect.

Lewis   Oh.

Waldorf   Cumggernaut. Sorry if that's a bit, you know.
Blunt.

Lewis   No.

Waldorf   Otherwise it can erm, hurt a bit. The end. The tip,
at the . . .

Lewis   Yeah right, well we won't use my phone then.

Waldorf   Cool. Though you know that was a really good
idea. Good initiative. Shown. By all. Here . . . with.

Silence.

Waldorf   So what now?

Lewis   . . . I don't know.

Waldorf   It's OK though.

Lewis   Yeah.

Waldorf   We'll work it out. All of it.

Lewis   Will we?

Waldorf   Somehow, yeah.

Lewis   Think I need a poo.

Waldorf   Good. Might help.

Lewis   How?

Waldorf   . . . I don't know, just do it, go on. (*Pause.*) Well go on.

Lewis   Yeah.

Lewis *exits.*

Waldorf   Why you locking the door?

Lewis (*off*)   What?

Waldorf   I heard you.

Lewis (*off*)   Oh, erm . . .

Waldorf   I'm not gonna come in. Unless you want me to (?).

Lewis (*off*)   No. Stay out there, please. But yeah, I will unlock it, if you want.

Waldorf   Doesn't bother me, just weird.

Lewis (*off*)   Sorry.

Waldorf   And stop fucking apologising!

Lewis (*off*)   Yep.

Silence.

Lewis *enters.*

Lewis   I couldn't go.

Waldorf   No. How about we take our tops off, to start the ball . . . ?

Lewis   . . . OK.

Waldorf   Yeah?

Lewis   Yeah. I will, if you will.

Pause.

Waldorf   Better.

Lewis   Is it?

Waldorf   Yeah. (*Pause.*) Nobody can see us, can they? From outside?

Lewis   No. Would it matter?

Waldorf   Suppose not.

Lewis   Filming it anyway.

Waldorf   Yeah.

Lewis   Then watching it in a tent full of hipsters.

Waldorf   Is that what they'll be like?

Lewis   Yeah, they'll be all hats and scarves and cheekbones. Can I turn the heating down?

Waldorf   Alright, yeah.

Lewis   I don't like to get too hot, while I'm . . .

Waldorf   OK.

Lewis   Yeah, I can . . . sweat a bit.

Waldorf   Really?

Lewis   Yeah, Morgan doesn't mind it, I don't think.

Waldorf   Sure. You been doing sit-ups?

Lewis   No.

Waldorf   Me neither. I should, really.

Lewis   Yeah. No, I like your shape.

Waldorf   Do you?

Lewis   Yeah.

Waldorf   You're not just shining my shoes?

Lewis   No. Always have.

Waldorf   Thanks.

Lewis   That's alright.

Waldorf   Well, I like your . . . your shape, too.

Lewis   You're just saying that now.

Waldorf   No. You know, looks: real.

Lewis   Let myself go a bit.

Waldorf   No, you're just: older.

Lewis   I look OK?

Waldorf   Yeah. More than . . .

Lewis   Thank you.

Waldorf   S'alright.

Lewis   Have you ever thought about me then? In like a dream, or?

Waldorf   No.

Lewis   OK.

Waldorf   What?

Lewis   Nothing.

Waldorf   Have you dreamt about me then? Like that?

Silence.

Waldorf   I mean I would dream about you.

Lewis   OK.

Waldorf   I just haven't, yet.

Lewis   Right. You don't need to pretend.

Waldorf   I'm not.

Lewis   I believe you.

Waldorf   OK. Dreamt about other guys.

Lewis   Who?

Waldorf   Remember Sick Dave? From Flat 2?

Lewis   Yeah.

Waldorf   Used to see him in the Halls' gym a lot.

Lewis   He was into his hockey, wasn't he?

Waldorf   Yeah.

Lewis   What were the dreams like?

Waldorf   . . . alright. Bit rough, actually. Quite rugged.

Lewis   Apparently it happens a lot.

Waldorf   What?

Lewis   Straight guys, sort of. Doing it. This. On film. We're not. The first.

Waldorf   Yeah?

Lewis   No. I did some research, online.

Waldorf   On your phone?

Lewis   Yeah. Gay guys seem to love it.

Waldorf   What?

Lewis   You know, the idea of someone giving in to something that . . .

Waldorf   They don't really wanna do?

Lewis   No, that they secretly want to, I think. There's loads of porn like it. Tons of it.

Waldorf   So what, it's gay guys pretending to be all straight and normal, then going gay coz it's all so wonderful and lovely and feels so wrong it must be right?

Lewis   The one I saw, yeah.

Waldorf   God, how do you act straight?

Lewis   He was wearing a baseball cap. Knee-length shorts. White socks. And he looked: genuinely nervous.

Waldorf   OK. Fair enough. Well we should say then, maybe, to the camera. That this is, just about us then. This isn't about other guys, you know. It's not. Gay. Or for, you know, the discerning gay, or whatever. Or hipsters.

Lewis   OK, yeah, maybe.

Waldorf   Is it?

Lewis   No.

Waldorf   It's not though, is it?

Lewis   No, it's just about . . . us.

Waldorf   Yeah.

Pause.

Lewis   We should maybe take our bottoms off, then.

Waldorf   All of it?

Lewis   Trousers. Socks, yeah.

Waldorf   Pants?

Lewis   What do you think?

Waldorf   Er . . .

Lewis   Leave 'em on? For the minute?

Waldorf   Yeah, go on.

Lewis   OK.

Waldorf   Sounds. Good.

Lewis   Let's do it.

Waldorf   Yeah. Probably best, if we close the curtains though. To be safe.

Lewis   Yeah.

Waldorf   We still recording?

Lewis   Yeah.

Waldorf   Well stop it. Delete it. I don't want all this on it.

Lewis   OK.

Waldorf   Or maybe, don't bother, actually. Leave it. We can edit it all out later on, can't we?

Lewis   OK.

Waldorf   Just leave it on, that way we won't miss anything, in case we suddenly start . . .

Lewis   What?

Waldorf   . . . like, you know, getting into it. Rutting.

Lewis   Alright.

Waldorf   You don't want to do it and then not have filmed it, do you?

Lewis   No.

Waldorf   'Nightmare (!).'

Lewis   Yeah.

Waldorf   *'Ye Gods, Jonathan!'*

Lewis   Yeah. (*Pause.*) I did this bit to camera, earlier. Before you got here.

Waldorf   How was it?

Lewis   Rubbish. Deleted it, right after.

Waldorf   What did you say?

Lewis   I don't know. Just rambling, really. Wanking on about . . . Not actually – wanking – just . . . We should get on with this.

Waldorf   Yeah.

Lewis   Do it.

Waldorf   Yeah.

Lewis   Just do it, now.

Waldorf   Yeah.

Lewis   Before we over-think it, or. Or talk about it too much.

Waldorf   Yeah.

Lewis   It's like pulling a tooth.

Waldorf   Is it?

Lewis   Yeah. Do it quick. Bit of blood. No fuss.

Waldorf   Right.

Lewis   No actually yeah scratch that . . . analogy. Fuck.

Waldorf   Yeah.

Lewis   I could get it out.

Waldorf   What?

Lewis   It.

Waldorf   That?

Lewis   Yeah.

Waldorf   Cock?

Lewis   Yeah.

Waldorf   Get your cock out?

Lewis   Yeah.

Waldorf   Right.

Lewis   Shall I?

Waldorf   Yeeeaaaaaaaaah, no. What . . . just through the boxers then, or . . . ?

Lewis   Yeah, or I could pull my boxers down a bit, for . . . ?

Waldorf   Either, is an option.

Lewis   Yeah.

Waldorf   Well it's up to you mate.

Lewis   Just might make it easier, if you see it first, maybe? Take the. Sting, out of it.

Waldorf   Really?

Lewis   Yeah.

Waldorf   . . . I'm not . . . not sure actually, mate.

Lewis   What about?

Waldorf   I don't know, I just . . . I just think that if I see it, right off, then . . .

Lewis   What?

Waldorf   That might not be for the best.

Lewis   Why not?

Waldorf   Well, just. Visually, you know, it's not very . . . is it?

Lewis   I know but maybe it will help. To get you into the . . . I could get it out now. Or you could just get yours out. I don't mind.

Waldorf   No.

Lewis   Alright, what about if we both get them out? At the same time?

Waldorf   No way.

Lewis   Why not?

Waldorf   Too: formal. Like, the Changing of the Guard.

Lewis   Alright. But maybe if we ease them off or out, gently. Then maybe move around a bit. With them both out. To, you know. Acclimatise. Gradually.

Waldorf   . . . but . . .

Lewis   Then you know, when we come in for the . . .

Waldorf   . . . kill?

Lewis   Yeah, when we come in for the . . . We'll be more. We'll know what we're dealing with.

Waldorf   I think I know what I'm dealing with mate.

Lewis   Yeah, but they're all different though, aren't they?

Waldorf   In size yeah, colour. Not in, basic, like. Design.

Lewis   Just a thought.

Waldorf   OK. Yeah, it's a good idea. But I thought, maybe, we'd . . .

Lewis   What?

Waldorf   Kiss. First.

Lewis   OK.

Waldorf   Is that a bit old-fashioned?

Lewis   No.

Waldorf   So what do you think?

Lewis   Yeah, it just might be harder, that's all.

Waldorf   Why?

Lewis   In a *Pretty Woman* sort o' way.

Waldorf   Who's Julia Roberts?

Lewis   Both of us.

Waldorf   Well that's a very different film then. So hang on what, we're not gonna kiss, at all?

Lewis   Well no, I don't wanna rule it out but . . .

Waldorf   So, you *don't* want to kiss but you do want us to get our cocks out and dance around the room lunging to acclimatise?

Lewis   I don't know. I don't know. I'm sorry.

Waldorf   It's alright. It's OK.

Lewis   Is it?

Waldorf   Yeah, just stop fucking apologising.

Lewis   (Morgan's always saying that.)

Waldorf   (Yeah. Great minds.)

Pause.

Lewis   OK. How about. Put your hand on it. On your own. Under your own like, boxers?

Waldorf   OK.

Lewis   Yeah, but look at each other. As we do it.

Waldorf   Right.

Lewis   That way we don't have to see anything. Yet. Or kiss, if that's . . . But we can . . . warm up.

Waldorf   Yeah?

Lewis   Yeah because you know, it's a tactile thing, isn't it? Famously.

Waldorf   Yeah.

Lewis   So I think that's the right thing to do, then.

Waldorf   OK.

Lewis   Let's do it.

Waldorf   Yeah. Just to clarify though: hand under the boxers? Not showing him yet? But maybe, moving him about a bit, in the paddock?

Lewis   Yeah.

Waldorf   OK.

Lewis   Ready?

Waldorf   Yeah. Bring it on. Lock and load. Let's. Roll (?).

Pause.

Lewis   So how's that?

Waldorf   . . . OK.

Lewis   Are you sort of cupping it or holding it?

Waldorf   Yeah.

Lewis   Which?

Waldorf   Both.

Lewis   And how does that feel?

Waldorf   OK. You?

Lewis   Yeah.

Waldorf   Cool.

Lewis   Yeah.

Waldorf   You sure? We can both stop, if you want?

Lewis   No. You?

Waldorf   I'm fine mate.

Lewis   Yeah?

Waldorf   Yeah.

Lewis   Just say the word, if you . . .

Waldorf   No.

Lewis   You're happy?

Waldorf   Yeah. Very much.

Lewis   You're not smiling.

Waldorf   I'm alright.

Lewis   OK. So what about. Now. Maybe. We start moving it, a bit?

Waldorf   Moving it?

Lewis   Yeah.

Waldorf   The hand, or the?

Lewis   Well . . .

Waldorf   What?

Lewis   Both.

Waldorf   Right.

Lewis   Just slowly. At first, maybe.

Waldorf   Yeah.

Lewis   Can you do that, do you think?

Waldorf   Right.

Lewis   Can you?

Waldorf   Right.

Lewis   You're just saying: 'Right.'

Waldorf   Am I?

Lewis   Yeah.

Waldorf   Right.

Lewis　So how about you move it then?

Waldorf　Move it?

Lewis　Yeah.

Waldorf　OK. Right.

Lewis　Slowly, at first.

Waldorf　OK. Right.

Lewis　Just a steady sort of.

Waldorf　Yeah.

Lewis　Ship. On the deep blue. Sea.

Waldorf　Steady. Ship. Blue.

Lewis　And maybe now a bit quicker, along the ocean?

Waldorf　Well . . .

Lewis　Like this.

Waldorf　Like that?

Lewis　Yeah, you doing it?

Waldorf　. . . yeah. I'm in the ocean, yeah.

Lewis　Are you?

Waldorf　Yeah.

Lewis　. . . you're not just moving your wrist?

Waldorf　No.

Lewis　Come on.

Waldorf　No, I'm doing it, alright?

Lewis　Good.

Waldorf　Yeah, I am.

Lewis　So are you getting anything?

Waldorf   Not sure.

Lewis   Feel it.

Waldorf   I am.

Lewis   Properly. Stop for a moment and . . . Yeah?

Waldorf   No. You?

Lewis   Nearly a . . . a semi, I think.

Waldorf   Really?

Lewis   Close.

Waldorf   Right.

Lewis   Is that alright?

Waldorf   Yeah. No. Well done mate. Congrats. Thumbs up . . . your . . .

Silence.

Waldorf   I'm really sorry.

Lewis   What?

Waldorf   I just need to . . .

Lewis   Waldorf.

Waldorf   OK. It's OK. It is. Give me a minute, OK?

Waldorf *exits.*

Silence.

Lewis   Are you alright?

Silence.

Waldorf *enters.*

Lewis   I didn't hear you . . .

Waldorf   Yeah, I didn't go.

Lewis   OK.

Waldorf   Maybe we should just . . .

Lewis   What?

Waldorf *kisses* **Lewis**.

Lewis *kisses him back.*

They kiss. Intimately. Slowly. For a while. They break off.

Silence.

Waldorf   We should fuck.

Lewis   Yeah.

Waldorf   Really?

Lewis   Yeah.

Waldorf   What's wrong? You don't want to?

Lewis   No, I do. I do.

Waldorf   OK, you just look like . . .

Lewis   Like . . . ?

Waldorf   . . . you don't.

Lewis   . . . no, I do.

Waldorf   Yeah?

Lewis   Yeah. I just . . . What if we . . . ?

Waldorf   What if we . . . ? What?

Lewis   What if we . . . ? I don't know, what if we . . . ?

Waldorf   Say it.

Lewis   . . . enjoy it?

Waldorf   Yeah?

Lewis   Yeah, what if we . . . ?

Waldorf   Like it?

Lewis   Yeah. Does that mean that we're . . . ?

Waldorf   I don't know.

Lewis   No, I don't.

Silence.

Waldorf   Are we still filming?

Lewis   Yeah. Light's on.

Waldorf   Good.

Lewis   Yeah?

Waldorf   Yeah. So you'd rather do it if you don't enjoy it, then?

Lewis   I don't know.

Waldorf   Coz I'd rather enjoy it.

Lewis   Yeah?

Waldorf   Yeah.

Silence.

Lewis   What about if we turned it off?

Waldorf   What?

Lewis   The camera.

Waldorf   Why?

Lewis   Well, er. We turn it off. We do it. We enjoy it, or not. That way. No one ever knows. Just us.

Waldorf   OK. But why still do it, if we're not gonna film it?

Lewis   I don't know.

Waldorf   What would you tell Morgan?

Lewis   I don't know.

Waldorf   Or Steph?

Lewis   I don't care mate.

Waldorf   You think we should though? Turn it off?

Lewis   Yeah, I do.

Waldorf   Right. Fuck.

Lewis   Yeah. What do you think?

Waldorf   I think you're right.

Lewis   Yeah?

Waldorf   Yeah. Though I don't know why. So OK then.
Turn it off.

Lewis   You're sure?

Waldorf   Turn it off, yeah.

Lewis   Alright.

Waldorf   Yeah. Fuck. You know?

Lewis   Yeah. Maybe, yeah.

Scene Two

Lewis, *alone*.

Pause.

Lewis   . . .

Pause.

Morgan *enters*.

Morgan   Sorry.

Lewis   No.

Morgan   Just needed to . . .

Lewis   Course. Totally.

Pause.

Morgan   Can't believe this place.

Lewis   I know.

Morgan   Like some . . .

Lewis   Yeah.

Morgan   . . . palace, or . . .

Silence.

Morgan   So quiet.

Silence.

Morgan   Right, well I'll go then.

Lewis   . . . no. Don't.

Morgan   What?

Lewis   . . . go.

Morgan   Why?

Lewis   So that we can . . . I just think . . . That . . . You and I . . . should . . .

Morgan   Lewis.

Lewis   Yeah. I can't quite . . . say, what I . . . You know?

Morgan   Yeah.

Silence.

Morgan   Don't really know why I'm here. Just odd being in the flat on my own on a, Saturday night.

Lewis   I'm glad you did. Come.

Morgan   Are you?

Lewis   Yes.

Morgan   Not sure I am. (*Pause.*) Lovely drive, though. All the grounds, lit up. Almost wish I was staying.

Lewis   We still could?

Morgan   Yeah. That's probably the worst idea I've ever, ever heard.

Lewis   Yeah. It is. I'm sorry.

Morgan   What for?

Silence.

Morgan   Is that the camera?

Lewis   . . . yes.

Pause.

Morgan   We could have a watch?

Lewis   I don't . . .

Morgan   Couldn't we?

Lewis   Morgan.

Morgan   Like a. Premiere. Got some Minstrels, in me bag.

Lewis   Just. Put it down. OK?

Pause.

Morgan   Alright. Whatever you want.

Silence.

Morgan   Are we just gonna stand here then?

Lewis   We could sit down?

Morgan   Yeah, that wasn't what I was . . . exactly . . . Was it?

Lewis   I know, no.

Silence.

Lewis   Morgan.

Morgan   What?

Lewis   Can I . . . say something?

Morgan   Please.

Silence.

Morgan   Well go on. (*Pause.*) Lewis?

Pause.

Lewis   Morgan.

Morgan   Say it.

Lewis   I will. I will. I will.

Methuen Drama Modern Plays

include work by

Edward Albee
Jean Anouilh
John Arden
Margaretta D'Arcy
Peter Barnes
Sebastian Barry
Brendan Behan
Dermot Bolger
Edward Bond
Bertolt Brecht
Howard Brenton
Anthony Burgess
Simon Burke
Jim Cartwright
Caryl Churchill
Complicite
Noël Coward
Lucinda Coxon
Sarah Daniels
Nick Darke
Nick Dear
Shelagh Delaney
David Edgar
David Eldridge
Dario Fo
Michael Frayn
John Godber
Paul Godfrey
David Greig
John Guare
Peter Handke
David Harrower
Jonathan Harvey
Iain Heggie
Declan Hughes
Terry Johnson
Sarah Kane
Charlotte Keatley
Barrie Keeffe

Howard Korder
Robert Lepage
Doug Lucie
Martin McDonagh
John McGrath
Terrence McNally
David Mamet
Patrick Marber
Arthur Miller
Mtwa, Ngema & Simon
Tom Murphy
Phyllis Nagy
Peter Nichols
Sean O'Brien
Joseph O'Connor
Joe Orton
Louise Page
Joe Penhall
Luigi Pirandello
Stephen Poliakoff
Franca Rame
Mark Ravenhill
Philip Ridley
Reginald Rose
Willy Russell
Jean-Paul Sartre
Sam Shepard
Wole Soyinka
Simon Stephens
Shelagh Stephenson
Peter Straughan
C. P. Taylor
Theatre Workshop
Sue Townsend
Judy Upton
Timberlake Wertenbaker
Roy Williams
Snoo Wilson
Victoria Wood

Methuen Drama Contemporary Dramatists
include

John Arden (two volumes)
Arden & D'Arcy
Peter Barnes (three volumes)
Sebastian Barry
Dermot Bolger
Edward Bond (eight volumes)
Howard Brenton
  (two volumes)
Richard Cameron
Jim Cartwright
Caryl Churchill (two volumes)
Sarah Daniels (two volumes)
Nick Darke
David Edgar (three volumes)
David Eldridge
Ben Elton
Dario Fo (two volumes)
Michael Frayn (three volumes)
David Greig
John Godber (four volumes)
Paul Godfrey
John Guare
Lee Hall (two volumes)
Peter Handke
Jonathan Harvey
  (two volumes)
Declan Hughes
Terry Johnson (three volumes)
Sarah Kane
Barrie Keeffe
Bernard-Marie Koltès
  (two volumes)
Franz Xaver Kroetz
David Lan
Bryony Lavery
Deborah Levy
Doug Lucie

David Mamet (four volumes)
Martin McDonagh
Duncan McLean
Anthony Minghella
  (two volumes)
Tom Murphy (six volumes)
Phyllis Nagy
Anthony Neilsen (two volumes)
Philip Osment
Gary Owen
Louise Page
Stewart Parker (two volumes)
Joe Penhall (two volumes)
Stephen Poliakoff
  (three volumes)
David Rabe (two volumes)
Mark Ravenhill (two volumes)
Christina Reid
Philip Ridley
Willy Russell
Eric-Emmanuel Schmitt
Ntozake Shange
Sam Shepard (two volumes)
Wole Soyinka (two volumes)
Simon Stephens (two volumes)
Shelagh Stephenson
David Storey (three volumes)
Sue Townsend
Judy Upton
Michel Vinaver
  (two volumes)
Arnold Wesker (two volumes)
Michael Wilcox
Roy Williams (three volumes)
Snoo Wilson (two volumes)
David Wood (two volumes)
Victoria Wood

For a complete catalogue
of Methuen Drama titles
write to:

Methuen Drama
Bloomsbury Publishing Plc
50 Bedford Square
London WC1B 3DP

or you can visit our website at:

www.methuendrama.com